D0562685

S'pose I Die

S'pose I Die

HECTOR HOLTHOUSE

THE STORY OF
Evelyn Maunsell

ANGUS
& ROBERTSON
PUBLISHERS

ANGUS & ROBERTSON PUBLISHERS

Unit 4, Eden Park, 31 Waterloo Road,
North Ryde, NSW, Australia 2113;
94 Newton Road, Auckland 1,
New Zealand; and
16 Golden Square, London W1R 4BN,
United Kingdom

This book is copyright.
Apart from any fair dealing for the
purposes of private study, research,
criticism or review, as permitted
under the Copyright Act, no part may
be reproduced by any process without
written permission. Inquiries should
be addressed to the publishers.

First published in Australia
by Angus & Robertson Publishers in 1973
Queensland Classics edition 1978
Reprinted 1981
Outback Classics edition 1985
This A&R paperback edition 1989

Copyright © Hector Holthouse 1973

National Library of Australia
Cataloguing-in-publication data.

Holthouse, Hector.
  S'pose I die: the story of Evelyn Maunsell.
  ISBN 0 207 16316 2.

  1. Maunsell, Evelyn, b. 1888. 2. Country life —
  Queensland. 3. Queensland — Social life and customs —
  1901-1945. I. Title.

994.304'0924

Printed in Australia by Australian Print Group

Contents

Map 1

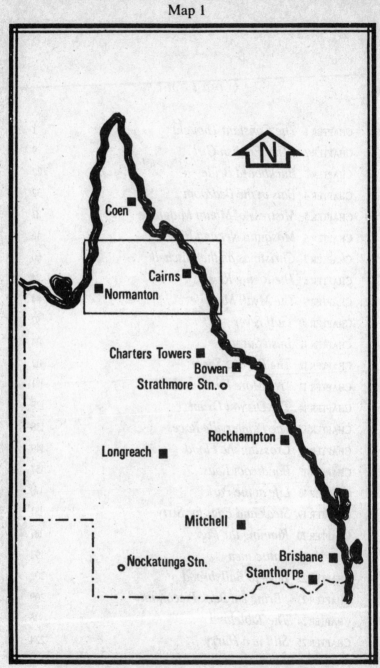

Queensland (the boxed area is shown in detail in Map 2)

Map 2

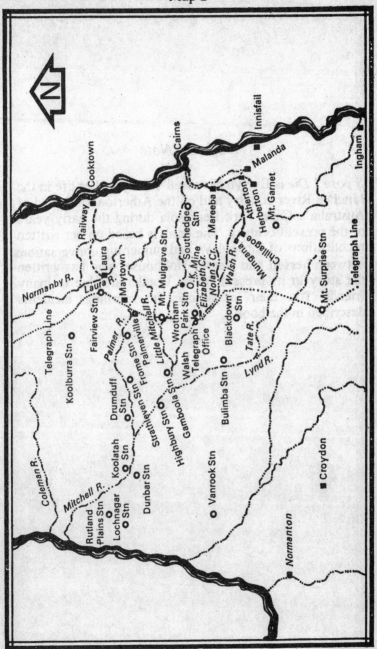

The Mitchell River and the Atherton Tableland

Author's Note

S'pose I Die is Evelyn Maunsell's story of her life in the
Mitchell River country and on the Atherton Tableland of
Australia's Cape York Peninsula during the early years
of the present century. The book is based on her written
recollections of those days and numerous conversations
between herself and Hector Holthouse, who has written
the story in its present form. Thanks are due to many
friends for their assistance in recalling incidents
described in the book.

CHAPTER ONE

❦❦❧

The Constant Thought

How long the time was when the musterers were away, the air heavy and muggy from the monsoon, the isolation emphasized by the meaningless chatter of the black gins coming from the kitchen. I tried to sit up in bed, but the fever and the miscarriage that followed it had left me so weak that the slightest movement was an effort.

It seemed an age since Albert, the Aboriginal house boy, had set up a bunk for me on the back veranda between the house and the kitchen where it was coolest. Since then I had been unable to get out of bed at all. A lot of the time I had been delirious, calling to the Boss, even though I knew he would not be home for another three weeks.

My movement must have attracted Albert's attention. He had never been far from me all the time I was sick.

"You all right, Missus?"

I tried to collect my thoughts to say something that I knew I must tell him. It had been nagging at me for days in all my lucid moments.

Malaria, or Gulf fever as they called it here in Australia's Cape York Peninsula, was a thing that was always with us when I came up in 1912 as the English bride of Charles Maunsell, manager of Mount Mulgrave cattle station on the Mitchell River. The Boss, as everyone called him, had grown up in this country and he regarded regular bouts of fever as a matter of course. I had come almost fresh from London, unused to the bush and unused to station life.

I had contracted malaria during my first summer here, and ever since had lived with the dread of having a bad attack of it while the men were out on one of their four-week mustering trips and I was alone at the homestead with only the black gins and Albert. The nearest white woman was twenty-five miles away, and with an infant of her own to look after and the wet-season rains turning the country into a bog, she would not have been able to reach me.

Now, after more than twelve months, the thing I had dreaded all along had happened. I had a bad attack of malaria while the men were away, and, to make it much worse, it had come just at the time when I was expecting my first baby.

The accepted treatment for malaria in those days was quinine, as much of the powder as would go on a sixpenny piece, dissolved in water and taken twice a day. There was nobody to tell me it was the worst thing a pregnant woman could take. Half delirious with fever, I dosed myself with quinine and brought on a miscarriage. Too weak to help myself, and with no one there to help me, I was sure I was going to die.

That was what had been on my mind all the days I had been lying here between spells of delirium—the thought of my dying and the Boss coming back from the muster and finding me after three weeks.

"Albert," I said, "maybe I die."

His eyes flew wide with fright, and quickly he shook his head.

"You no more die, Missus. You no more die."

But there was no reassurance in his words. All they meant was that he could not face the prospect. That was always the dreadful part of it; although the blacks were there, you were still so much alone. Faithful old Albert would have done anything for me, but at a time like this he was helpless. Somehow I had to make him understand what needed to be done.

"Albert," I said, "s'pose I die, you dig a hole and put me in it, and cover me up, and tell Boss I bin lose em piccaninny."

The possibility of death was a thought we had with us constantly in the Peninsula in those days. Less than sixty years ago it was still untamed country, with large cattle runs, managed often by one white man with a few black stockmen, and no other white inhabitants within twenty-five, fifty, or even a hundred miles, except perhaps a few old diggers still scratching in the gravels of abandoned gold diggings. During the wet season rivers and creeks spread out miles wide, and flat country between them became a bog so soft that a horse would sink to his belly in it.

The Mitchell River rises in the eastern part of Cape York Peninsula in the Great Dividing Range just north of Cairns, and flows 350 miles westward to the Gulf of Carpentaria. Most of the rain that feeds it falls during the monsoonal months of the year, but it discharges more water than any other northern Australian river. Its tributaries include the Lynd, Tate, Walsh, Hodgkinson, and Palmer. Many creeks break away from its main stream, some to lose themselves in dry country, some to find their way back at last to the parent river, others to make their own way to the sea.

In places its course is flanked by long, deep lagoons covered with water-lilies, and its sandy bed is dotted with flat islands providing ideal nesting sites for crocodiles. It is a beautiful river, with a clear running stream all the year round, many deep reaches of still water, and banks covered with thick scrub and a great variety of vines and creepers.

The higher reaches gather their waters from the gullies and gorges of rugged mountains of the Great Divide, the middle reaches channel the broad black-soil valleys of the cattle country, and the lower reaches meander over the vast flats of the Peninsula's western shores where, more than a hundred miles from the nearest mountain, floodwaters of January, February, and March break low banks to spread out and become a vast, shallow sea surrounded by miles of boggy ground in which nothing can move. Musterers caught on these flats in the wet often perish, cattle drown in hundreds.

Frank Simpson once told me how his wife had gone with him to Lochnagar Station, near the mouth of the Mitchell, as a nineteen-year-old bride in 1915. When she was expecting her first baby towards the end of November he took her in the buggy with two black gins, and some black boys riding beside, and started off on the trip south to Normanton, a hundred and fifty miles away. Within a few days heavy rains forced them back.

During the next three months they tried again and again to get through, but each time met vast seas of water and had to return. They made it at last, about the end of March, after a three weeks' roundabout trip over two hundred miles of flooded country. Rivers were crossed by swimming the horses and floating the dismantled buggy over piece by piece in a boat made out of a tarpaulin. Mrs Simpson was ferried over in the same way, but for many miles she plodded through the mud. Her baby was born a few weeks later.

The Mitchell was discovered by Ludwig Leichhardt in 1845 on his expedition from Brisbane to Port Essington, and named after Sir Thomas Mitchell, Surveyor-General of New South Wales. Leichhardt reported good grazing country along his route and cattle-men began to follow in his tracks. Among them came men like Philip Sellheim, who took up Strathmore Station on the Bowen River where my husband Charles grew up, and Ernest Henry, who roamed the north looking for likely land in company with Rudolph Morisset. I knew Morisset when he was an old man and he used to tell me how he would camp on a promising block to see that nobody else took it while Henry rode in to Bowen to register a claim to it.

Hard times in the 1860s slowed the settlers down, but by the early 1870s gold-rushes to Ravenswood, Charters Towers, and other northern fields provided a market for beef, and a great northward surge of cattle began.

Following reports of gold on the Palmer River, the prospector James Venture Mulligan and his party in June 1873 came up through Mount Surprise Station. They crossed the Tate and then the Waish, which they followed down, fording its tributary, Elizabeth Creek, on the way, until they reached the Mitchell, a strongly flowing stream about two hundred yards wide. Crossing it with some difficulty, they continued north past the limestone peak of Mount Mulgrave to the Palmer, where they found enough gold to start Queensland's most spectacular rush.

Pat Callaghan, a sixteen-stone, six-foot-four Irishman from County Limerick, was in the north at the time with a gang of men and two bullock teams supplying posts for the overland telegraph line that was being pushed up the Peninsula towards Cape York. He got as far as Elizabeth Creek and his men deserted him to rush to the diggings. Pat, making the best of a bad job, took his two bullock teams to the Palmer, slaughtered them, and sold their stringy meat to the diggers for top prices, paid in gold fresh from the river. The price was so good that he lost no time in going into partnership with a butcher, Tom Leslie, and two cattle-men, Jack Duff and Jack Edwards, to provide a regular supply of meat for the diggings.

Callaghan did the buying, paying for his cattle with gold that he carried round with him in chamois-leather bags and weighed out as needed on scales from his saddle-bag. As holding stations for the partnership's cattle, he took up a number of blocks of land along the Palmer and Mitchell rivers. One of these was my future home, Mount Mulgrave, stretching from the Mitchell to the Palmer across Mulligan's old track and taking its name from the mountain.

The new gold-rush was bringing more cattle-men in its tracks, and among the new stations formed was Wrotham Park on Elizabeth Creek, where I spent some of my happiest years in the north. It was formed by A. C. Grant, who brought three hundred head of Skene and Henderson's fat cattle from Havilah Station, on the Bowen River about 380 miles to the south-east. It took its name from Wrotham, Skene's home town in Kent, and George Henderson, who had been in the butchering business in New Zealand, was granted the lease on 16th June 1874.

On the Palmer River, downstream from the goldfields, Willy and Henry de Sallis, who had already bought Strathmore Station, took up and stocked Strathleven. Edward Palmer, John Stevenson, and Walter Reid took up Gamboola on the Mitchell below its junction with the Walsh.

The gold-diggers were soon consuming beef at the rate of about twenty thousand cattle a year at prices up to £10 a head. As fast as one goldfield was worked out, others were found—at Maytown, up the river from Palmerville, on the Hodgkinson, on countless creeks and gullies of the Mitchell system, and north over the Great Divide almost to the tip of the Peninsula. Wherever the gold led diggers, the cattle-men went also.

North of the Palmer the country was almost unknown, crossed only by Edmund Kennedy, who had been speared to death by Aborigines in 1848, and the Jardine brothers, Frank and Alex, who had fought a pitched battle with the blacks near the mouth of the Mitchell in 1864. Against odds that seemed impossible the cattle-men moved into it—men like Pat Fox, who used to say his homestead consisted of whatever his packhorse could carry, men with no money and so few cattle that they complied with stocking regulations by moving the same mob from one block to another. The blacks fought them every foot of the way.

Two drovers bringing cattle up to Strathleven were surprised at night in their camp on Wrotham Park and battered to death. Native Police tracked the killers down, found them celebrating on stolen beef at Corroboree Swamp, about five miles from the homestead, and shot the lot.

In 1881 George Bristow, managing Gamboola, was speared through the left lung and found by Billy Wilson, manager of Mount Mulgrave, lying on his front veranda in a pool of blood. Wilson broke off the end of the spear, sat him on a horse, and took him fifty miles to the hospital at Maytown. He eventually recovered sufficiently to return to Gamboola and manage it for another sixteen years.

Harry Jones took up Koolburra Station, on the North Kennedy River about forty miles north-west of the diggers' staging camp of Laura, in 1880 and was shot in his sleep soon after by his fourteen-year-old black boy. Police found the boy with his tribe and took him to Cooktown, where he was acquitted because of his youth and returned to his tribe. The boy had wanted to go walkabout, so had waited until Jones was asleep, taken his revolver, and shot him.

After that Koolburra was bought by Jimmy Collins, a good cattle-man and excellent horseman who was generally known was "Terrible Jimmy" because he was so hard on the blacks. They developed a healthy respect for him and had a big corroboree to celebrate his departure when he sold out to Pat Fox and Pat's two nephews, Jim and Ernie.

When my husband Charlie was managing Koolburra as a young man in 1907 the blacks were still as hostile as ever and he had several narrow escapes.

The Cape York telegraph line, providing the Colony's oversea link through Thursday Island, was completed in 1886. Upkeep was difficult because the blacks regularly raided it for wire and porcelain insulators, both of which could be made into good, sharp spear points.

Rutland Plains Station, in the midst of the network of temporary streams south of the Mitchell's mouth, was taken up by Frank and Archer Bowman about 1903. On 26th August 1910 Frank, then aged forty-five and alone on the station with his family, was ambushed by a Mitchell River

Mission native and hit in the temple with a spear tipped with a three-inch nail. He shot the blackfellow, but died of his wound a week later.

Nearly two years afterwards, when I arrived at Mount Mulgrave, the station blacks were still talking about the spearing of Bowman. Mrs William Lakeland who was cook at Mount Mulgrave, told me Mrs Bowman had to bury her husband, read the burial service over him, and then pack up and drive with her young children and a faithful black boy more than a hundred miles to the nearest neighbour.

Mrs Lakeland herself had grown up in the Mitchell River country and her husband, Billy, an old gold-rush mate of Pat Callaghan's, had spent most of his life prospecting in the Peninsula, discovering a number of small goldfields, including Coen.

Billy died in 1920—a death as lonely and isolated as much of his life had been. While riding from Coen to Iron Range, more than eighty miles farther north, something went wrong and he perished. His remains were found and identified from his saddle and other articles three years later. Some of his mates clubbed together for a headstone, which was carved at Cooktown, taken to Laura by train, and then dragged up to his lonely grave through some of the roughest country of the Peninsula on a horse-drawn sled made out of the forked branch of a tree.

Pat Callaghan met his death in 1911 as a result of a bizarre accident. Ever since his early days in the north he had slept with a revolver under his pillow. The precaution had saved his life on a number of occasions when he was attacked by blacks, and he had never got out of it. One morning, after sleeping on the veranda at Mount Mulgrave homestead, he was rolling up his blanket when the revolver fell out onto the cement floor, went off, and shot him through the heart.

It was Pat Callaghan's death that was responsible for my meeting the man I married and coming to live in the Mitchell River country myself.

CHAPTER TWO

⋘⋙

"*This English Girl*"

The important things in my life have always happened in a hurry. When my mother knew I was coming my father went pedalling off on a penny-farthing bicycle to fetch Dr Shemell, who lived about two miles away, but before they were back in the doctor's brougham I had already arrived and was yelling lustily.

That was 21st October 1888. My mother was twenty-three and the only help she had was from her maid Sarah, who was twenty-four. I was christened Evelyn Violet and grew up in our two-storey brick home in St Mary's Road, Ilford, then a township of about eight hundred people on the outskirts of London.

The doctor who had arrived too late was a German. I remember him as a kindly, snowy-haired old gentleman dressed in a long black frock-coat with astrakhan collar and a tall beaver hat. He always took off his hat at the front door, deposited it upside down on the hallstand box, and dropped his kid gloves into the box before coming into the drawing-room. If we children had only minor complaints we would be waiting there for him in front of the big coal fire. I have always remembered the fires we had in England. In the kitchen there was a big range which was kept burning day and night, and there was a two-hundred-gallon tank connected to it with pipes running upstairs so we had hot water for our baths.

I had two elder brothers, Rupert and Fred, and after me came brother Aubrey, sister Ida, and three younger brothers, Hugh, Ralph, and Basil. We were a united family and did everything together.

The Roding River ran through Ilford and as children we collected watercress along its banks. Under the trees that grew beside it was a little factory, with only two rooms, which used to make photographic plates—the forerunner of the huge Ilford photographic factory that stands there to-day. The Royal Mail coach used to pass through the town on its run over the old Roman road to York, and it made its first stop to change horses at the White Horse Hotel. The change took just five minutes and we children used to wait there to watch it.

My father was an active supporter of the Conservative Party and I remember the wild excitement of election nights when all the townspeople waited up for the coach to come through with the results of the poll. Everyone wore huge ribbon rosettes—red, white, and blue for the Conservatives or Tories, and yellow and black for the Liberals or Whigs. As soon as the votes were counted in London our winning candidate and his supporters would take a coach out along the York Road, calling at all the town halls and climbing up on the balconies to declare the poll.

It was always midnight by the time they got to Ilford, but we would still be waiting for them as they came clattering down the street in the four-in-hand with the candidate sitting beside the driver in top hat, and a man on the back of the coach blowing a trumpet.

At the time of Queen Victoria's Diamond Jubilee in 1897 I was nine years old. My father, who was an importer, had his office at Cheapside on a first floor with big glass windows overlooking the street, and I was taken as a special treat to see the royal procession. I remember Queen Victoria sitting alone in an open landau, stately and dignified, dressed in black and carrying a sunshade. Then came the Royal Family, including the Prince of Wales, who became King Edward VII, great-grandfather of the present Queen. They were followed by the Indian princes, resplendent in magnificent jewel-studded robes and turbans. The Lord Mayor of London followed in his gold coach, and then soldiers from different regiments all over the British Empire. The procession took an hour and three-quarters to pass.

Before she left Buckingham Palace that morning the Queen had signed twenty-five commissions for officers in the army and volunteer forces. One of them was for Captain Frank Evans, my father.

It all made an indelible impression on the nine-year-old girl I was then. Looking back on it now, over three-quarters of a century, it seems like part of a totally different world.

The first I ever heard of a place called Queensland was when staying with Grandpa and Grandma Evans. Grandma's people were a Scottish family called Nicholson and they had always been Presbyterians. When she was a little girl they went to listen to a follower of John Wesley's preaching on street corners, and after hearing his fiery exhortations they all became Methodists. Three of her brothers migrated to Queensland as Methodist missionaries.

Grandpa Evans was a Welsh herbalist and he used to send us children out along the brooks and over the meadows collecting medicinal herbs that grew there. We would walk for miles and bring back huge bunches of them. I remember white nettle was one of the main ones. Grandpa used to boil them up and then strain the liquid. He would boil down pig's fat and mix the herb extract with it to make ointments. Everything had to be carefully packed and labelled and we used to help him. I remember thousands of little wooden boxes he kept his remedies in, and the testimonials he had from Harley Street doctors.

As we grew up my brother Rupert became an accountant and also joined the King's Colonial Regiment, hoping it would give him an opportunity of seeing Australia, Fred took a commission in the City of London Regiment, and I was apprenticed to a French millinery firm in London. My father by then was a major and an Alderman and Freeman of the City of London. All the family led a very active social life and my girlhood became a gay round of military balls, banquets, and other official occasions.

I went to many of the balls with a young lieutenant named Reggie Grimwood, and I think most of our friends and family took it for granted that one day we should be married. But all my family seemed to have an adventurous streak in them, and even as children we used to talk of going to the colonies and making a home there for mother and father.

Rupert was the first to go. He had worked in London for Bergl Australia Limited. They gave him a letter of introduction to Mr Thomas Hall, who was chief accountant for the New South Wales Railways, and he sailed in 1910, working his passage as baker's mate. In Australia Rupert worked with Mr Hall for a while and became friendly with Hall's three sons, Arthur, Harry, and Frank, but he soon took a position on Bindi Bango Station, in northern New South Wales, to get experience on the land.

With Rupert's letters coming home about life in Australia, I soon decided I too was going to see more of the world, though my father was very much against it. I was a single girl, only lately turned twenty-one, and in those days girls simply did not do that sort of thing. My main ally was my mother. "I'd trust my two daughters anywhere," she used to say.

My chance came when my Aunt Rosebelle wrote to say that Mrs Dean, a wealthy friend of hers who had three married daughters in Australia, New Zealand, and South America, was going on a two-year world cruise to visit them all and needed a companion. It was a chance of a trip round the world, and luckily for me there was no time for anybody to argue.

On Tuesday morning I met Mrs Dean in London and agreed to accompany her. She was leaving England that Friday, which meant that my luggage had to be packed and at Tilbury dock in time to be aboard the S.S. *Osterley* by Thursday evening. Mrs Dean and I were to travel by train to Marseilles and pick up the ship there for Sydney where one of Mrs Dean's daughters lived. My father was terribly worried because none of us knew anything about Mrs Dean. Rupert would not be able to meet me in Sydney, so I wrote to his friend Harry Hall, who was married and lived near Sydney, and asked him to meet me at the ship.

Then a big cabin trunk was bought and everything was packed into it and another trunk, both were sent off to the ship, and by 8 a.m. on Friday I was at Victoria Station with two golden sovereigns my father had given me in my purse, and all the family and friends—there were twenty-seven of them, including Reggie Grimwood—to be fare-welled on what we thought was to be my trip round the world.

It was a gay send-off, in spite of a few tears, and as the train began to gather speed the last I saw of my family they were all lined out along the platform waving me out of sight. I remember calling out to Reggie Grimwood, "If I don't meet anybody nicer than you, I'll come back to you, Grimmie."

Everything was new to me from then on. The train drove straight onto the ferry at Dover, and off onto the French railway system at Calais. A few days in Paris, a few more in Marseilles, and we boarded the *Osterley* for Australia. Mrs Dean bought me a basket of violets and a bottle of French perfume to send to my mother and looked after me like a daughter all the way to Australia. The only money I had was the two golden sovereigns my father had given me, and the fifteen shillings a week I received from Mrs Dean, but she took me everywhere first class and I wanted for nothing. We arrived in Sydney in April 1911 and Harry Hall and his wife Maude were at the wharf to meet me.

Thomas Hall had an orchard at Thornleigh, just north of Sydney, and his sons Harry and Arthur had their own homes on the property. Mrs Dean did not need me while she was with her daughter and I spent a good deal of time with the Halls.

Arthur had married a Miss Frances Maunsell, and when I visited them I met her widowed mother, Mrs Jane Maunsell, and a younger daughter, Phoebe. The Maunsells were station people from the north, and there was a son, Charles, who was head stockman at Nockatunga, a cattle station in the Channel Country of south-western Queensland. I saw a good deal of Mrs Maunsell, and it was she who gave me my first insight into the kind of life women lived on the more remote Australian stations in those days.

Her father, Dr Macansh, a British Army surgeon, and her mother had been killed in the Indian Mutiny in 1857, after they had sent Jane and her two sisters to the doctor's brother John and his married sister, Mrs White, at Canning Downs Station, on Queensland's Darling Downs. In 1868, while at Canning Downs, Jane met and married Samuel Maunsell, a former Royal Navy midshipman, who took over the management of Talavera Station, on the Balonne River in southern Queensland, where there were no other white women within miles.

Their eldest daughter, Frances, and two sons were born there, and while Samuel was out mustering all three contracted dysentery and both boys died. The station black boys and gins helped Jane dig graves for the two little boys and bury them, she herself reading the service. Then she had a fortnight to wait for her husband to return so she could tell him his sons were dead and buried.

Samuel and Jane left Talavera after that, and it was while Jane was staying with her sister at Walloon Station, about 130 miles west of Bundaberg, that Charlie was born at the near-by town of Banana. In 1883 Samuel went to manage Strathmore Station, about sixty miles south-west of Bowen, in northern Queensland, and she and the children joined him there. While they were at Strathmore another daughter, Phoebe, was born.

Strathmore belonged to Willy and Henry de Sallis, who also owned Strathleven Station, on the Palmer River west of Palmerville, and Samuel regularly had to ride more than four hundred miles across country to Strathleven to bring back cattle. For company on these trips he had only his black boys and a Chinese cook named Jimmy Ah Say, son of an old Palmer gold-rush digger. I later knew Jimmy when he came to cook at Wrotham Park Station. I also knew Ah Quay, another of Samuel's old cooks.

Once while Samuel was away Jane was sitting inside with young Charlie, who was sick, when the terrified house gin came running in to say that three Murries (wild black-fellows) with spears and boomerangs, were at the door demanding tobacco. Jane snatched up a gun, and when they saw it the Murries ran. But as they went each of them spun round and flung a heavy fighting boomerang. One boomerang flew harmlessly over Jane's head, another stuck deep in the wooden door of the meat house near by, and the third buried itself in the gin's chest, piercing her lung, so that she died soon after.

Samuel died in March 1899, aged only fifty-nine, and four years later, when Frances married, Jane and Phoebe came to live with her at Thornleigh.

My brother Aubrey followed me to Sydney in September 1911, working his way out as a steward, and planning to get a job on a station. In those days a man working his passage signed on for the single trip only, and received no wages, so when I met him at the wharf one of the first things I asked was, "How much have you got?"

"Fifteen shillings," he said.

"I've got five," I told him.

We took a cab to Thornleigh and Harry Hall gave Aubrey a job scrubbing and packing lemons so he could earn enough money to get out into the bush.

Towards the end of 1911 Jane Maunsell told me her

son Charlie had been offered a position as manager of Mount Mulgrave Station, on the Mitchell River in the far north of Queensland, and that he was coming down from Nockatunga to see her in February before taking up the new job. Such visits were rare. He had come to see her about twelve months earlier, before going to Nockatunga, but before that she had not seen him for about ten years. Jane was very excited when she gave me the news and it was the only time I ever remember seeing her smile. She had the saddest face I have ever seen.

Everyone was looking forward to the visit and I caught some of the excitement. Charlie had to come past where I was staying on his way to his mother's place and I was keeping a look-out for him. I do not know what I was expecting, but I had never been out in the bush and I was used to seeing men properly dressed in suits.

Charlie had come across country from Nockatunga and finished the trip by train to Thornleigh railway station where his young nephew, Tom Hall, met him with a billy-goat cart to carry his luggage. As he came walking past beside the cart—this tall, thin man, still in his dusty bush clothes—I was not at all impressed and I said to Maude Hall, "If that's Phoebe's brother, she can keep him."

But when Aubrey and I and the rest of us went over to meet him that night he was all cleaned up and dressed in a new Anthony Hordern's suit, and looked quite different. He was twenty-eight at the time, and a typical bushman— six feet two and a half inches tall, lean and straight as a Guardsman, with fair curly hair and a complexion tanned by a lifetime in the bush. We all went to town to see *Our Miss Gibbs*. There is a character in the play called Tim, and from that time on Charlie insisted on calling my brother Aubrey "Tim", so there was nothing for the rest of us to do but follow suit. There was something about the name Aubrey that the bushman in Charlie could not take to— they were all Jack, Dick, and Tom where he came from.

I had never met anyone like him before, and the way

he talked about life in the outback made it all seem like an exciting adventure. At Nockatunga he had lived in a homestead built of mud from the Wilson River which ran only every few years after heavy rains, temperatures rose to 120 degrees Fahrenheit, storms were of dust instead of rain, and they bred their own camels.

Some people would probably say it was love at first sight with Charlie and me—if they liked to forget about the time I first saw him go past. I had soon found that in spite of the bush clothes he was every bit as much a gentleman as the silk-hatted and morning-coated young men I had been used to in London, and the fact that he had only a week in Sydney before going back to the bush for perhaps another ten years left no time for delay in making up our minds. In any case, within a few days I had made another of my quick decisions, and we were engaged and talking about wedding plans.

Charlie had been sixteen when his father died and, there being no other white man on the station, he had to do everything for his father himself, including making a coffin and burying him. After that he had taken a job in a bank in Bowen for four years to keep his mother and two sisters. There were no pensions in those days. Only after his sister Frances was married to Arthur Hall and his mother and Phoebe had a home with them had he felt free to take his first bush job as book-keeper and jackaroo at Lyndhurst Station, about 160 miles west of Townsville near the head of the Einasleigh River, and then owned by Mr J. H. S. Barnes. But he still sent every penny he earned to his mother, living himself on the rations and quarters provided by the station.

"We can't get married for a long time," he told me at one stage. "I have to look after mother and Phoebe and I haven't got any money. I had to break in twenty horses at two pounds a head up at Nockatunga to get money to make this trip to Sydney."

He received £2 5s. a week wages on Nockatunga and the owner, Maddock Hughes, gave him a £50 bonus when he left. His salary as manager at Mount Mulgrave was £4 a week and keep. But by that time I had decided such a good son would also be a good husband, and I was prepared to rough it with him. If we were married, I told him, the station rations and accommodation would be good enough for both of us, so what more did he want?

Then he wanted to be married at once so I could come north with him at the end of the week. But, though I never had a moment's hesitation about marrying Charlie, that idea did not suit me at all. Most of my relations had been against my leaving England alone as I had done. I remembered the way my mother had backed me up, and I would never betray the trust she had put in me. I was not going to give anyone a chance to suggest that I had to get married in a hurry.

I told Charlie he would have to write for my father's consent in the proper way. So he wrote to my father, and I wrote to my mother saying I wanted to marry an Australian bushman and go and live with him on a cattle station. I am afraid neither of us mentioned our financial situation. My poor parents were going to get quite enough of a shock as it was.

There was no air mail in those days, and getting my father's reply from England was going to take more than three months. Meanwhile, up at Mount Mulgrave, the fat bullocks had to be mustered and on their way to the meatworks by the end of June, because after that the feed began to go off and the cattle to lose condition. Mount Mulgrave was rough country and mustering it took months. There was no chance of Charlie's extending his stay in Sydney. It was decided at last that he should go north and do the muster while I waited in Sydney. My brother Tim followed him later to get some of that bush experience he had come to Australia to acquire.

I had to write to Reggie Grimwood and break the news of my engagement, and Charlie, who was also engaged, had to break his journey at Rockhampton to tell a girl he had known up north on the Palmer River that he was going to marry an English girl instead of her.

I do not know what she thought about it all, but in due course I got my letter from Grimmie. "I knew you would do that," he said. Not a word of reproach. Poor old Grimmie, he served in both world wars and was taken prisoner in each.

Meanwhile, my eldest brother, Rupert, had come to Sydney from Bindi Bango to see me, become engaged to Phoebe Maunsell, obtained a position as an accountant with an estate agent in the town of Mitchell in south-western Queensland, and left to establish a home there for Phoebe and for her mother, who was to live with them. He asked me to come up to help with the furnishing of the house, and while there I met Mrs Ashton Murphy and her husband, who, though now better known for his drawings in the Sydney *Bulletin*, was then postmaster at Mitchell. Mrs Murphy was very kind and insisted on making my wedding dress for me.

My father wrote to say, "I suppose this young man is the one you want; by the sound of him he is quite a decent sort of fellow." My mother approved. My brother Tim wrote from Mount Mulgrave to tell me he had painted the station homestead for me and was coming south to stay with Rupert. Charlie wrote to say he was busy on the bullock muster and as soon as he got them on the road he would wire me to book my berth on a ship from Brisbane to Cairns.

The wire came in July: "Arranging wedding Cairns 21 July or close as possible. At Imperial Hotel from Monday. Advise date of arrival. Love. Charlie."

My first glimpse of Cairns was on 18th July 1912 as the S.S. *Morialta* steamed slowly up the Trinity Bay channel with all the passengers lining the rails forward to watch the approaching shoreline. Although it was the middle of the Australian winter, the day was hot and muggy, and the cloud-flecked sky a shimmering blue. On the southern shores of the bay forest-covered hills dropped straight down to the sea. Ahead was the town itself. Compared with London and Sydney it hardly looked like a town at all— just a cluster of buildings on a low-lying shore with jungle-clad mountains behind.

The main thing in my mind was something that had been worrying me throughout the whole of the five-day voyage from Brisbane. Would I recognize Charlie again when I saw him? I had known him for only a week at Thornleigh, and that was five months ago. Would he be the same sort of man in these strange surroundings? As the ship swung in towards the wharf I was trying to pick the tall figure I remembered from among the crowd. But there seemed to be tall men everywhere, a few in suits, but most in the kind of bushman's clothes Charlie had been wearing when I first saw him. The ship nudged gently against the wharf, the heavy mooring cables went over the side, and still I could not see him. I was close to panic.

The gangway banged into position. It was hardly settled against the ship's side when a tall figure, in the same Anthony Hordern's suit he had worn when I first met him, came bounding up two steps at a time. I need not have worried about recognizing him.

The first of Charlie's friends I met was Dick McManus, estate agent and executor of Pat Callaghan's estate. It was he who had written to Charlie asking him to come and manage Mount Mulgrave. I had seen the letter with the flourishes of the flamboyant "R. T. McManus" signature covering more than half the page:

Cairns, 13 December, 1911

Mr C. G. Maunsell

My Dear Sir:
    You will have heard of Mr Callaghan's tragic death, and will, I think, hardly be surprised when I ask you what you would be prepared to accept to take complete charge of Mt Mulgrave and Frome (the

Mt Mulgrave out-station), with of course, an efficient assistant staff.

With kindest regards,
Yours Very Sincerely,
R. T. McManus.

McManus, then about thirty, and handling the business of many of the northern stations, was already a man of considerable influence in Cairns. He received me graciously and quickly put me at ease, but apparently had his private reservations. I learnt later that he had said to a friend, "I'll have to look around for a new manager; this English girl will never stick it out at Mount Mulgrave."

CHAPTER THREE

❦

Buckboard Bride

Dick McManus had a horse cab waiting at the wharf and we drove to the Imperial Hotel where Charlie had booked a room for me. Cairns seemed to be a pleasant little town with wide streets, big shady trees, and gardens massed with bright flowers, but it was quite different from any other town I had known. Clusters of tall coconut palms rose above the horizon and most of the back gardens seemed to have thick clumps of broad-leafed banana plants and other tropical fruit-trees growing. In the distance I could see pineapple plantations and canefields.

I was interested in all these things because at home in England we had grown our own vegetables and always had plenty of them both winter and summer. We had a glasshouse for things like tomatoes and cucumbers in the cold weather, and I had always been determined that one day I would have a vegetable garden of my own.

The Imperial Hotel was run by the Fox sisters—Mrs Emma Hoare, whose husband later became mayor of Cairns, Mrs Florrie Connors, and Nellie and Paulina. Paulina was engaged to Dick McManus.

After I was comfortably settled in Charlie told me the plans he had made. "We're being married the day after tomorrow, Dick will give you away, and Paulina will be bridesmaid. The Fox sisters are giving the reception at the Imperial."

All the arrangements for the wedding seemed to be complete, and we were to be married in St John's Church of England by the Reverend Mr Tomkins at 4 p.m. on 21st July. Dick McManus said he had ordered a carriage and the best pair of greys in town to take me to the church. Charlie wanted to know if I approved of the arrangements.

"The arrangements appear to be very nice indeed," I told him. "But you seem to have forgotten the most important thing of all. Have you heard from my father yet? I will not be married without his consent."

They both laughed uproariously as though this was a great joke, and when they were finished my father's letter to Charlie was produced. Charlie had had to get a special licence for the marriage because I was not arriving in Cairns until just before the date he had set, and I never heard the end of that special licence. It had cost £2 5s. and Charlie used to joke about it for years after. "You can't do just as you want around here," he used to tell me. "You cost me two pound five shillings, and you'll do as you're told." He only had £5 to get married on, and that extra £2 5s. really got him.

I shall never know how I got through that day before my wedding, there was so much to do. My dress, at least, was ready. Mrs Murphy had made it beautifully, based on a style fashionable in London at that time, but modified to suit the Queensland climate. It was ankle length, of sheer linen with lace insets and ruffles on the skirt and bodice. The sleeves were elbow length, and at the high neckline I planned to wear a brooch my mother had given me before I left home. The hat I had made myself, of stiffened hailspot net with ruched silk round the crown and a silk bow at the side.

Although I knew not a soul in town, everybody seemed to know all about me, and I seemed to be meeting people all the time who told me they had known Charlie for years.

The hotel was packed that week-end. There was a long passage of single rooms which they called the Alley, and these were let to the young bank clerks, public servants, and other single men about town, who were called the "Alley Boys" in consequence. They were a happy, high-spirited crowd and, as everybody knows everybody else's business in the north, they knew all about my being English, about my whirlwind engagement, having to wait for the muster to finish, and everything else. They thought it was one huge joke. They gathered in the passage outside my room singing songs and making up amusing verses all that Saturday morning while I was getting ready for the wedding.

The little church was packed. The women's dresses, a lot of them from Sydney fashion houses, were mostly crisp, cool-looking voiles. The one my bridesmaid, Paulina Fox, wore was a lovely grey-blue. The men all wore lightweight woollen suits and did not seem to feel the heat at all. I was not used to the tropics and I felt it terribly. The church was hot and at the crowded reception I felt I was stifling.

Among the uninvited guests were, of course, the Alley Boys, who had all brought their own drinks and were making a day of it, though they were so entertaining they were as welcome as anybody.

All this time I had not seen one familiar face on my wedding-day except Charlie. Then, towards the end of the reception, a young man who had been at militia practice arrived still resplendent in his blue-and-red uniform. I did not notice him at first, but he apparently had one long look at me and then pushed his way through the crowd to Nellie Fox to ask who I was.

"That's Mrs Charles Maunsell; you've just missed her wedding."

"Yes," he persisted, "but who was she before she was married?"

"Evelyn Evans, she's an English girl."

"Evie!" he exclaimed. "It's young Evie. I went to school with her at Ilford."

He came pushing across the room to where I was standing. "Ernie Radford," I cried. It was so good to see a familiar face. His sister Mabel had been my best friend at school and I had often visited their home. I had not even known he was in Australia, but the thing that mattered most was that his was the one face from home that I saw on my wedding-day.

After the wedding breakfast there was just time for Mr Sunners to take my photograph on the balcony upstairs before I got ready to catch the train. My going-away dress was a white linen, tailored in Oxford Street, which I had brought with me from home, and with it I wore a black hat trimmed with plaited blue, pink, and mauve ribbon. Though the outfit was the most suitable I had for the occasion, I still felt the heat, though by now it was late afternoon. Dick McManus found my discomfort amusing.

"Call this hot?" he demanded. "Wait till you get up there on the Mitchell."

Our honeymoon was to be one day at Kuranda, a mountain resort overlooking Cairns, followed by a 240-mile journey by train, buckboard, and buggy to Mount Mulgrave. The train left about 6 p.m., which, in the tropics, left us enough daylight to look round us as we ascended the Barron River Gorge to the tableland.

The range had a huge cleft in it through which the Barron River tumbled on its way to the sea just north of Cairns. Up the forest-clad slopes of this gorge the railway line ran over high trestle bridges, along steep embankments, and through innumerable tunnels, becoming steeper and steeper as it neared the top.

Charlie told me that when he was leaving the north to go down to Nockatunga, the season was wet and Number Nine tunnel had caved in, so all the passengers had to get out and walk about a mile round the tunnel through thick tropical jungle to where another train was waiting for them. They had a dead man on the train with them and all the men had to take turns carrying him.

Sunday was our honeymoon at Kuranda before we continued our journey to Mount Mulgrave where a lot of work remained to be done before the wet season set in. That morning we walked down a jungle path to the Barron Falls where the waters of the river tumbled 770 feet on the first part of their descent to the coast from the Atherton Table-land, and it was here I had my first chance to see the man I had married in his proper surroundings. Charlie loved the bush and he moved about in it as part of it. He knew all the different kinds of trees and why they grew the way they did. He pointed out the orchids and bird's-nest ferns that grew high up in their branches, and told me the names of the birds I could hear twittering and whistling all around us.

Nothing would satisfy him but that we should climb down to the bottom of the falls and see them from there, I tried, but the slope was steep and the ground slippery from spray, and before long I had to sit down and wait while he went on alone.

First thing on Monday morning we caught the train for the 140-mile trip to the inland railhead of Mungana. Once we got away from the thick rain-forest of the range, the bush was open and dry-looking with masses of golden wattle in bloom, and huge, bulbous anthills among the trees.

It was a funny little train we were in, terribly slow after those of England and France, and mostly goods, with one carriage for passengers divided into two compartments, one for first-class passengers, one for second, and each big enough to hold only about ten people sitting in two seats facing each other.

It made me think of the day I left London on the boat train for Paris on the first stage of my trip to Australia. The first-class railway carriage had eight compartments, each reserved, and all lined with white kid. Mrs Dean's, with a little card in the window saying "Mrs Dean, Miss Evans", had been decorated by her groom with white heather. In the compartment next to us was the Marquis of Londonderry.

Our little train kept stopping to drop off mail at tiny stations consisting of one small galvanized-iron shed. There seemed to be more of them than I could count, but I remember Lappa Junction where Chris Quinn was station-master and his wife gave us a very welcome cup of tea.

At Chillagoe Mrs William Atherton and her three daughters, Essie, "Chum", and "Bob", were on the platform to welcome me to the district. William, Jack, and Ernest (generally called Paddy) Atherton were the three sons of John Atherton, the man who explored and opened up the Atherton Tableland. Ernest represented the Table-land in the Queensland Parliament and became Minister for Mines.

I remember, some time after this first meeting, when Chum Atherton and I were joking she said to me, "What were you doing, taking the nicest man in North Queens-land?"

"What were you doing letting me?" I asked. "I only knew him for a week; you northern girls knew him for years."

Chum herself married one of the nicest men I have ever known, Dr Jarvis Nye, who practised on the Tableland for many years.

About dark that Monday night we arrived at the end of the line—the copper-mining township of Mungana, a cluster of galvanized-iron houses and a galvanized-iron hotel where we put up for the night.

I had never seen anything like that hotel. It was a long building, divided off into tiny rooms by galvanized-iron partitions no more than six feet high. You could almost look into the next room and everybody in the building could hear everything that was said. Most of the others staying there were miners, who were in and out at all hours of the night, and some of the language was very colourful and in-formative to a girl who had never been in the bush in her life.

Mungana was always a terribly hot place, and that first time I was there the miners all trooped in for dinner at night in grey flannel shirts with short sleeves and sweat rags round their necks. The smells of the sweating men, the cooking and the spilt drinks, all in that oven-like iron building, were almost overpowering.

There was no ice-chest, of course, and no such thing as a cold drink. But I was fortunate in that the manager of the copper-mines, Mr Rhodda, had a table specially set aside for him, and he very kindly invited us to join him there. He had his own ice-chest, and next morning at breakfast he had ordered a papaw for me, ice cold, freshly cut open, and flavoured with sherry.

We had been met at Mungana by Tom Graham, the Mount Mulgrave odd-job man who had come out to take us the remaining eighty miles in the station buckboard. This buckboard was a four-wheeled vehicle pulled by two horses. There were no springs on the axles, only a pair under the seat which went across the body near the front, and there was no hood to keep off the sun. Swags and gear, including my big cabin trunk, were piled in the back behind the seat.

Everything was ready for us to move off when two young girls drove up in another buckboard and said they were Jessie and Eliza Ferguson from Blackdown Station, about forty miles to the west of Mungana. They had been up at four o'clock that morning to milk a herd of about forty cows and deliver the milk to the Klondyke copper-mine. Then they had driven on to Mungana to invite us to drive home by way of Blackdown because their mother wanted to welcome me to the district. The girls were twins about my own age, twenty-three, and they thought nothing of the work they had done that day before most people in the city would have been stirring.

So we made a detour through the bush to Blackdown where we were received by Mrs Ferguson, a very gracious lady whose husband had worked in a bank in Victoria before deciding to go on the land. She had accompanied him all the way north to the Peninsula and helped him build up Blackdown in untouched bush country.

Mrs Ferguson had three sons and, as well as Jessie and Eliza, there was an elder daughter named Minnie. After her husband died she and the children carried on the station alone, the boys, as they grew older, taking other jobs to bring in extra money.

We stayed at Blackdown two days, and when Mrs Ferguson heard that I had worked in the West End she asked me to show her girls how to do their hair in the latest London fashion. We tried, and had a lot of fun about it, but the girls would not take the thing seriously. What use was a London hair-style in the bush, and what time would there be to look after it with forty cows waiting to be milked at four o'clock every morning?

Mrs Ferguson would not hear of my going on to Mount Mulgrave in the buckboard, but insisted that we take her little Abbott buggy. This was a small type of buggy with a hood and good springs, so the trip was much more comfortable from there on. Mrs Ferguson came with us as far as Wrotham Park Station, while Tom Graham took the buckboard on ahead with a Cingalese cook named Sin Sin Yu, whom Dick McManus had engaged for us at Cairns.

We heard later that when Tom arrived at Mount Mulgrave they all crowded round the kitchen table and asked him, "What's she like"? Tom held up the big white enamel teapot and said, "She has a skin just like this." My English complexion had been something quite new to him.

Much of this Mitchell country consisted of vast, treeless plains covered with high grass and dotted with big magnetic anthills, taller than a man and flattened out with their broad sides facing east and west and their points north and south. There were also round, dome-shaped ones, which were often broken up and mixed with water to make good hard floors for station buildings, and other little pointed ones, no more than a foot high. There were patches of scrub, and the plains were broken by sand ridges and lagoons surrounded by thick tropical growth which attracted all kinds of birds, including brolgas and pelicans.

From Blackdown it was about twenty miles north to the wide sandy crossing of the lower Walsh near the Telegraph Station. Fred Emerson was in charge of it at the time and Mrs Emerson made me very welcome and sent me on my way loaded up with bottles of jam and chutney she had made from her own fruit, and all kinds of bush recipes for me to try. Not far from the station I noticed a fenced-in grave which they told me was that of Mrs Tom Gardner, wife of Emerson's predecessor.

A seven-mile drive to the east along Elizabeth Creek brought us to Wrotham Park Station where we stayed the night. Wrotham Park was managed by Billy Evans, and after dinner he and his wife played us a number of records on an old cylinder phonograph, including "Home Sweet Home", which, of course, sent my mind straight back to all my family at Ilford. Life on the Mitchell was going to be very different from that.

Everyone at Wrotham Park kept impressing on me that Mount Mulgrave was "not like this". Mrs Lakeland, who had been cooking for Pat Callaghan, was still at Mount Mulgrave, and Mrs Billy Wilson had gone there as a bride while her husband was managing it, but I gained the impression that the place was still rather primitive. I told them about my plans for the garden and before we left in the morning Mrs Evans loaded the buggy up with cuttings of roses and begonias, and also a lot of mango seedlings.

On the track next day I asked the Boss, as Charlie was called in this part of the country, what the homestead at Mount Mulgrave was really like.

"It's a very nice little house," he said. "Not quite such a comfortable place as Wrotham Park, but there's a beautiful river full of fish, and we'll get to work and make a nice home of it."

All along the road I had noticed that whenever the name "Bowman" or "Rutland Plains" was mentioned someone looked at me and frowned and they changed the subject. I wondered what it was all about, but as no one seemed anxious to tell me, I did not say anything. I was to find out soon enough when we arrived at Mount Mulgrave.

A good distance out from Wrotham Park we stopped to boil the billy at a place called Lee's Grave, where a man named Lee had died and been buried. It was a tea-tree flat with a waterhole, and the water was so muddy the tea they made from it came out of the billy the colour of ink. I could not drink it.

"What's wrong with the water?" I asked.

"Oh," said the Boss nonchalantly, "a mob of weaners have just passed through; they always stir the mud up a bit."

At Lee's Grave there were mud springs where the fine, sloppy mud oozed up out of the ground and formed little hills. Years later, in 1936, the Boss took some geologists to look at them, and these experts said there were signs of oil there. But there was not much interest in oil in that part of the country in those days, and nothing was done about it.

About ten miles farther on we came to the Mitchell River crossing with good clear water running over a sandy bottom. About half a mile upstream on the northern bank, on a rise so that it looked out across the river, was Mount Mulgrave homestead.

CHAPTER FOUR

❧❧❧

Bats in the Bedroom

Tom Graham and all hands, boys, gins and piccaninnies—
a crowd of thirty or so—were waiting at the big double gates
leading into the house yard to see the "new Missus belonga
Boss".

I was dusty and tired, feeling strange and a little lost in
the unfamiliar surroundings, and as soon as the first greet-
ings were over I was handed over to the care of an old black
gin named Maggie, with a head of hair tousled like a mop
and a clay pipe clenched between her white teeth, and
dressed in nothing but an old shirt that came barely half-
way down her thighs.

She led me across the veranda and into the bedroom,
cement floored, with walls of unlined galvanized iron
recently painted by my brother Tim, and bare rafters under
the iron roof.

The first thing Maggie said to me was, "He bin spear
em all right."

"Speared who?" I asked, not being able to connect the
statement with anything I knew of.

"Him bin spear em Mr Bowman."

That was how I learnt what all the silence had been
about at the different stops on the way out. Everyone knew
that I would be left alone for weeks at a time, just as Mrs

Bowman had been at the time of the spearing. I do not know why Maggie came out with it like that. Probably someone had told her not to tell me about it and, half-wild old myall that she was, she reasoned that I would especially want to know.

I asked Maggie to show me the bathroom so I could have a shower and clean-up. It was a little galvanized-iron box of a building on the upstream side of the house, partly closed in by walls about five feet high. The shower was a bucket affair which you filled with water and then raised up over your head with a rope over a pulley, and tied there. When you pulled a string it lifted the plug out of the bucket, and that was the shower. The toilet was about a quarter of a mile from the house—a huge pit, about six feet deep, with galvanized iron round it.

By the time I had cleaned up it was nearly dark and I only had time for a quick look at the house before we sat down to dinner. It was built of corrugated iron on a frame of pit-sawn timber, and consisted of two rooms, each about twelve feet square, and a twelve-foot-wide veranda surrounding them. The whole had a cement floor.

The kitchen was a separate building on the downstream side of the house, with an antbed floor and surrounded by a veranda adjoining the veranda of the house to make an open, covered area where the men had their meals. On the two corners of the veranda farthest from the kitchen were two little rooms of galvanized iron, not much more than six feet square and of little use for anything.

The only white woman there was Mrs Lakeland, then about fifty-three, a strange, rather formidable person, quite unlike anyone I had ever known before. She had been a girl of fourteen when gold was discovered on the Palmer River in 1873, she had grown up in the midst of the rush, and had married Billy Lakeland, a prospector who spent much of his time looking for new fields. Her son and daughter were born and reared on the Palmer, and when I met her they were at school in Cooktown and Billy was somewhere in the far north looking for gold. Self-sufficiency and independence were the core of her character. She had her own horses, saddles, and plant. Having spent most of her life among men, she spoke like a man. She could shoot like a man and look after herself as well as a man.

As soon as I met her Mrs Lakeland told me her swag was packed and she would be leaving in the morning. She had nothing against me, but she had never worked with another woman before and she was not going to start now. I explained that I had come almost straight from London, that I knew nothing about the bush, and that I would be very glad of her help, if only for a week. I could have saved my breath. She had made up her mind to go, and go she would.

Dick McManus's brother Paddy had been looking after the station until the Boss arrived to take over, and had left before I arrived. Paddy was what they called a "veranda boss"—he did most of his supervising from the house. He did not like salt beef and he had eaten all the fowls on the place and drunk all the liquor. He did not get along with Mrs Lakeland, and because of this had introduced "inside" and "outside" eating at Mount Mulgrave for the first time. He had the table set inside for himself. Mrs Lakeland and the men ate on the kitchen veranda.

When Pat Callaghan was alive all the white people ate together with Pat at the head of one big table like an old-time patriarch, surrounded by his staff and maybe a friend or two who were passing through, or a cattle buyer, the mailman, a travelling priest or minister, with Finlay, his half-caste lad, whom some believed to be his son, sitting on the floor beside his chair.

Callaghan was a good talker, everybody called him Pat, and meals at Mount Mulgrave in those days were happy affairs. Finlay, before being given his dinner, would be asked to recite his antecedents on his father's side. The list always began with the name Macpherson, and then went on to include the name of every man who had ever worked on the station, present dinner guests, and always ended with "Callaghan".

Finlay had a half-sister, aged about nine, who was a full-blood Aboriginal. She always managed to pick up and repeat more gossip than all the other blacks on the station put together.

The regular white staff at Mount Mulgrave when I arrived consisted of the head stockman, Johnny Seibel, whose father had been a butcher on the Palmer River during the gold-rush, and Tom Graham, the odd-job man, who looked after fences, brought in the firewood, rations and so on, and when not otherwise engaged went out with the musterers as cook.

In addition there were a number of old-timers whom Pat Callaghan had known since the gold-rush days. He had let them make the station their home and given them all jobs to do for their tucker. One of these men was a former officer of Native Police, Rudolph Morisset, a son of Lieutenant-Colonel J. T. Morisset, one-time Commandant of the Norfolk Island convict establishment. He dined inside with us. The rest were outside.

Mrs Lakeland had prepared us a very nice dinner that night, and we ate it in the dining-room—just the three of us, the Boss, myself, and old Morisset—by the flickering light of a kerosene table lamp. After dinner I asked the Boss to take me out the back to meet the men. It was dark by then and there was not much to see by, just a hurricane lantern hung between the two verandas and a fat lamp in the kitchen.

The men had put on their best white shirts in honour of my arrival. Normally they wore flannel shirts like the Mungana miners or navy blue with white stripes. They were sitting on long forms on either side of the table and all stood up when I came out, but sat down with me when I took a seat on one of the forms. Their talk was mainly about dried-up waterholes and cattle getting bogged, but they were all good-humoured and joking, a bit rough and tough, but nature's gentlemen every one of them.

Mrs Lakeland did not go out of her way to tell me anything or show me anything. I do not know what part of the house had been her quarters before the Boss and I arrived, but when I asked her where she was sleeping that night she said the kitchen veranda would do her, and I did not see her again until she came to say good-bye. I think she had lived so long in the bush without having a woman's company that she did not want a woman around. I nearly got to that point at times when I was quite satisfied with my surroundings.

Charlie and I retired early that night, he carrying a hurricane lantern to light the bedroom, which was in pitch blackness. The only warning I got was a flurry in the gloom of the rafters, and then the whole room was full of them—a horrible horde of squeaking, fluttering, leathery-winged bats. They were no bigger than mice, but they were everywhere, blundering into my face and trying to cling to my clothing so I could not get away from them. I was terrified. I had never seen anything like it. But the Boss was quite unconcerned.

"It's only the light that's disturbing them," he said. "They sleep in the rafters. They'll settle down as soon as we put the light out."

They did settle down slowly, after we put the light out, but their squeaking kept up all through the night. I hardly slept at all. Tired as I was, I could not stop thinking about all that had happened since my wedding no more than a week ago. All the people I had met on my brief honeymoon had been so kind, but their lives were completely different from everything I had been used to. My mind kept slipping back to my family and home in Ilford where my father left for work every morning dressed in a frock-coat, a tall silk hat, and gloves.

Then there would come a flurry of wings and a fresh outbreak of squeaking among the bats in the rafters, and in the distance I would hear the sounds of corroboree drifting over from the blacks' camp on the still night air—high-pitched voices and the droning and clicking of their strange, savage music, as the boys and gins celebrated the coming of ''New Missus belonga Boss''.

CHAPTER FIVE

❧⟶

Mistress of Mount Mulgrave

In the morning Mrs Lakeland appeared, ready to leave, in divided riding skirt, shady, broad-brimmed hat, and a pair of men's elastic-side boots. Her horse was saddled, her rifle in the saddle holster, and her pack animals loaded. She said her good-byes briefly, swung herself onto the horse's back, and rode off, sitting side-saddle, heading out for Cooktown two hundred miles away.

The last thing she said to me was, "Don't let that bougainvillea die; I brought it from Cooktown."

That bougainvillea and one solitary lime-tree near the bathroom were the only things growing at the house when I arrived. I had asked the men at breakfast if there were any fresh vegetables. "There's some pigweed out the back," said the Boss.

He showed it to me later, a green patch of a low-growing sort of succulent that had spread over the damp ground where the kitchen slops were normally thrown out. On a lot of stations in those days pigweed was the only green they had. People ate it to help keep off the scurvy induced by a constant diet of salt beef and damper.

There was a weed they called Prince of Wales Feathers growing down by the fence along the river. It was a sort of wild spinach, fit to eat if there was nothing else, but not very appetizing.

In Pat Callaghan's time Mount Mulgrave had been so famous for its green vegetables that men would work there for lower wages than at other stations because of the good food. The Boss said the vegetables had to be planted on the river flats as soon as the floods went down after the wet, and that we would be able to start our vegetable garden after Christmas.

Mrs Lakeland's departure left me with a lot to learn in a hurry. The kitchen was a galvanized-iron shed with three-foot-wide wooden work benches along two walls and, across one end of it, a huge cooking range that had been salvaged from the O.K. mine township about thirty miles away to the south-east of us on the southern side of the Mitchell. The firebox, big enough to take a log of wood that would burn all night, was in the middle with ovens on either side of it, each twenty-four inches wide, fifteen inches deep, and four feet from front to back—large enough to take a whole batch of bread. A big hot-water urn always stood on top of the stove.

During the day the Boss showed me round. Near the kitchen was the meat house, a small room with walls extending about three feet up, and the rest of it, including the door, completely gauzed in to keep out the flies. Inside was a work bench and a big chopping block.

There was a harness shed, a blacksmith's and work shop, and, most important of all, the store. Inside was as black as pitch until the Boss unbolted and opened the shutters. "Got to keep the place bolted," he explained. "If there are any wild blacks around, the store is the first place they make for."

Inside, the room was packed with goods like a general store—six months' supplies of food, clothing, and every-thing else needed for the station. In the wet season nothing on wheels could move, so rations were ordered from Burns Philp and other traders in Cairns, and railed to Mungana, where Tom Graham picked them up in the wagon.

The winter loading had arrived about a month before I came, and there were a lot of items, sent by Dick McManus, that were marked not to be opened until I arrived. There was a case of tinned fruit, a case of tinned crab meat, a large case of Bulldog stout, and a whole lot of other little delicacies. There was also a roll of fifty-two yards of cretonne with a note from Paulina Fox pinned on it saying, "To ceil the place."

Remembering those bats, I was inclined to agree that the house certainly needed ceiling, but cretonne was not my idea of the right thing to do it with, though I found out later that a lot of the early bush homesteads were ceiled with cretonne. Anyway, I decided to wait until we could get timber, a decision I regretted later.

I never altogether got used to those huge orders we had to give every six months. I kept our order for the following October, and I still have it.

There were four tons of flour in fifty-pound bags, one ton of coarse salt, one bag of fine salt, twelve seventy-pound bags of sugar, one bag of brown sugar (for spiced beef), one large case of tea, two twenty-eight-pound cases each of dried raisins, currants, and sultanas (I was later able to add to our ration by making our own candied peel), twenty pounds each of cream of tartar and carbonate of soda, two cases of mixed jams, one case (two hundred two-pound tins) each of treacle and golden syrup (the latter generally known as bullocky's joy), six bags of Japanese polished rice, three bags of Chinese unpolished rice (packed in matting), one large cask of curry powder, two ten-pound cases each of dried apricots, peaches, prunes, and apples, one fifty-pound sack of dried peas, one sack of potatoes, one sack of brown onions, one case each of Holbrooks and tomato sauce, one small case of lemon and vanilla essence, twelve pounds of hops, and two cases of one-ounce packets of Epsom-salt.

In addition to food the order listed two forty-two-pound cases of plug tobacco, one case each of wooden and clay pipes, and two large cases of Bell and Black's wax matches, each case containing 144 dozen packets and each packet containing twelve tins of matches. There were four cases (or eight four-gallon tins) of kerosene for lighting and medicinal purposes, four dozen fishing lines, and one box of mixed fish-hooks.

As well as all this, there were items like one dozen hobble chains, one dozen each of different-sized buckles, ten packets of horseshoe nails, four pounds of beeswax, five balls of twine, sides of different weights in leather for making new harness, twenty-four yards of saddle cloth, yellow serge for the lining of saddles, blankets, material for gins' dresses, and all kinds of other things.

There was always a big order of boots, shirts, and trousers of all sizes. Each black boy received two pairs of riding boots and trousers and two shirts every six months.

We used a lot of leather because everything was done with horses in those days and there was a lot of harness. Peter Cameron travelled from station to station doing harness repairs. The stockmen used to make their own whips and spent hours plaiting them, covering the stocks with a strip of kangaroo hide, and making the crackers from stranded silk or horsehair.

Counter-lining a saddle was a more complicated job and only an expert could do it properly. Constant use packed the horsehair saddle padding so hard that it had to be taken out about every twelve months and replaced with fresh hair, which had been specially coiled and teased out to make it soft and springy. The way of doing it was to get a bundle of horsehair and coil it by putting a brace and bit into it and winding it up into a tight ball and tying it. Then it was boiled to soften it and, still coiled up, thrown on a galvanized-iron roof to dry. When dry it could be teased out into perfect padding, curly and springy, and ready to be pushed carefully under the saddle lining with a stick. The Boss, like most real bushmen, always preferred to do his own counter-lining, though he showed me exactly how it was done. He always said his mother was very good at the job.

Mount Mulgrave, like all the northern stations at that time, relied mainly on local black boys to do the mustering work, and they generally became very good horsemen and stockmen. They signed on by putting a thumb-print on the contract, and from then on they took their orders from the Boss and he found everything for them. He gave them their clothing and rations and looked after them when they were sick. He did the same for their families, too—their gins and piccaninnies, their relations and hangers-on. In addition to their keep they were entitled to a small wage, which the employer paid to the Government.

The blacks had their camp away behind the black-smith's shop. Most of the humpies were built of anything the owners could lay their hands on, but a few who were useful with their hands had asked the Boss for some iron and timber and he had helped them build quite comfortable huts.

All of them came to the kitchen for their food, which they ate at a bench under an iron roof outside the gate of the house yard. Every Sunday they lined up at the store to draw their week's ration of soap, matches, tobacco, and maybe a new fishing line, pipe, or something else they needed. The gins all had dilly-bags woven from bark stripped off the roots of certain trees, and they carried these by a sort of band across their foreheads with the bags hanging down on the back of their necks, and stuffed with fishing lines, soap, pipe, tobacco, matches, and a mass of other things they always carried about with them.

Once they had their rations the gins and piccaninnies all trooped off down to the river to swim, fish, and skylark about for the rest of the day. Some of their menfolk joined them, catching fish with six-foot spears tipped with three prongs of sharpened fencing wire. They caught all kinds of fish in the river, including barramundi up to thirty inches in length, and also quite a few venomous water-snakes, of which the gins were more frightened than of anything.

Others of the boys returned to their camp, stripped off

their civilized clothes, took up their spears and boomerangs, and went hunting. They were a happy lot, those station blacks, and you could always hear their laughter around the place. They were well fed and looked after, the boys worked hard and willingly when they needed to, and they knew how to relax and enjoy life when they had a spell.

The Boss took me down to the river to watch the fishing. The Mitchell at the homestead was a large channel between eighty-foot banks, and though this was the dry season it was still running strongly over a broad, sandy bottom. Out in the stream there were a lot of sandbanks and little islands on which, the Boss told me, you could often see crocodiles basking in the sun.

The Boss was a very good rifle shot and he told me that when he worked on Mount Mulgrave in Callaghan's time he and Pat had often shot crocodiles from the homestead veranda. They were the small freshwater kind, growing to no more than about six feet in length and supposed to be quite harmless. The gins and piccaninnies swam among them without any concern, though they generally kept clear of the nests, which were made in the sand. Each nest contained dozens of eggs which hatched out before the wet in time to let the young ones grow big enough to look after themselves before the river flooded.

Later that day Maggie's three-year-old piccaninny, Robin, came to me with a whole squirming, snapping hatful of these baby crocs, thrust them under my nose and said, "Here, Missus, you take em."

There were saltwater crocodiles, too, in parts of most of these northern streams, and they were a different proposition altogether. They grew to twenty feet in length and northern people generally called them alligators to distinguish them from the smaller kind.

As a boy Charlie was watching a bullock drinking at a waterhole in the Bowen River, a few miles from Strathmore homestead. Just as the animal finished and turned to leave, an "alligator's" tail came sweeping out of the water and knocked it into the mud where the reptile seized and drowned it. Charlie and his father used to hunt out their nests in the mudbanks and smash the four-inch-long eggs and hatching young ones with sticks.

In the afternoon the Boss took me for a row up the river and down again past the homestead to the rapids about a quarter of a mile farther downstream. The Mitchell was a beautiful river, with rich alluvial flats ideal for growing corn and vegetables, and high, tree-lined banks on either side. The homestead was situated on a rise on the northern bank, so we had a view from the veranda both up and down the river.

Though the area round the house was bare and dusty when I arrived, the bush trees were lovely and had huge clumps of orchids growing up among their branches. There were masses of wildflowers in the bush, too—ground orchids, white everlasting daisies, and pretty little blue flowers shaped like the English snowdrops I had often gathered at home.

Sunday was mail day at Mount Mulgrave. Percy Parsons, the mailman, our main contact with the outside world, would arrive with the mail from Mungana about four o'clock in the afternoon, stay with us overnight, and move on next day, taking our own letters with him. I could hardly wait for the mailbag to be opened that first Sunday, with its letters from home and the English papers my father sent me. There were also the Australian papers. All the stations got the *Cairns Post*, the *North Queensland Register*, *Queenslander*, and Sydney *Bulletin*.

There were no roads over most of the mail-run and mail and a few small parcels were all the packhorses could carry. Anything bigger had to wait until we could send into Mungana for it. In the wet season the mailman came to the opposite bank of the Mitchell River—when he could get that far—and somebody would go across by boat to collect the Mount Mulgrave and Gamboola mail. A black boy would ride over from Gamboola to collect theirs.

On Monday morning the men were out getting ready for a trip north to Frome, the out-station on the Palmer River run by Herb Doyle, and I settled down to picking up the threads of running a station homestead.

I soon found that Sin Sin Yu, the cook from Ceylon, knew nothing at all about cooking on a station. He could not make bread, one of a station cook's most important jobs, and he had no idea at all what to do with salt beef that had been dried and smoked until it was so hard that you could knock a man out with it. There were no eggs because Paddy McManus had eaten all the fowls, and there was not a thing in the vegetable garden. Without Tom Graham I do not know how I could have got through those first few days. He showed me how to soak the meat overnight to make it soft enough to cook. He made a damper for the midday meal, and he helped prepare the dinner.

Tom tried to teach Sin Sin Yu to make bread, but soon gave up and showed me instead. It was simple enough once you knew how. Before starting on the bread you had to make your own yeast by pouring boiling water over two tablespoons of hops, when it was cold adding two tablespoons of flour and two of sugar, bottling the mixture in a well-seasoned bottle, and allowing it to work for twelve hours.

The bread was made in an old tub—so many sieves of flour, enough water to make a stiff dough, yeast, and last of all salt. The tub was covered with a blanket and stood near the fire overnight. In the morning the dough was kneaded and worked well and put back in the tub until midday. Then it was kneaded into loaves, put in the tins to rise, and when risen baked in a hot oven. Before long I was making some of the best bread I have ever tasted.

Another of my jobs was making all the soap that was used on the station. A five-pound tin of caustic soda was dissolved in about three-quarters of a four-gallon kerosene tin of water and slowly stirred into four gallons of melted fat that had already been strained through muslin, and the whole boiled gently until converted into soap. It was then poured into a tub to set, and when hard tipped out and cut into bars with a wire which had a stick at each end of it to serve as a handle. It was quite a simple recipe, but one had to be very careful when adding the soda to the fat to see that the mixture did not boil over.

My main help in the house was old Maggie, who had been around the place for years. Pat Callaghan had never taken much trouble to train her, and by the time I arrived there was not much I could do. She was a real old bush myall, used to doing one or two jobs and incapable of learning any others.

One of her jobs was to look after the antbed floor of the kitchen by swabbing it down every morning with a mop made out of a fifty-pound sugar-bag wrapped round a stick. She could rake up leaves around the house and kill snakes, but that was about all. She never did anything without being told, and her real day began after the midday meal was over and she could make off down to the river to go fishing.

One of the first things I did was to make Maggie a proper dress. There was a treadle sewing machine in the house, and in the store I found a roll of Turkey red twill and another of striped navy-blue and white galatea. My pattern was simple—just a yoke of the Turkey twill, and the galatea skirt hanging loosely from it.

There was plenty of unbleached calico in the store, and from this I made myself dresses to wear about the station. All my good clothes I stored away carefully in my cabin trunk so I would always have something nice to wear when the occasion called for it.

I made red and blue dresses for the other gins in the camp, too, and white ones of unbleached calico for them to wear on Sundays. They looked much better in proper dresses than they had in the old shirts and things they had generally worn before I came, though the men sometimes joked about it, and said it was easy to see that Mount Mulgrave had a woman around the place at last.

CHAPTER SIX

❧❦❧

Mosquito Net and Rifle

There was always a lot of mustering to be done at Mount Mulgrave. It was shorthorn country, and the bullocks were mustered for sale during the first part of the year when they were in good condition from feed brought on by the wet. In the dry season, during the latter part of the year, there was more mustering to keep the cattle on water.

The only permanent water on Mount Mulgrave was in the two rivers that bounded it—the Mitchell on the south, and the Palmer on the north. In between were creeks, gullies, and lagoons which were filled by the wet-season rains but went dry in the winter. As they dried out the cattle had to be mustered back to one or other of the rivers for water. Sometimes early storms would fill the lagoons and tempt them away, but by then the country was so dry the water would soon soak away. The cattle did not have enough sense to find their own way back to the rivers, and they had to be mustered back.

Pleuro was always a problem on northern runs and cattle had to be inoculated against it. In those days before the introduction of the syringe this was done by pouring the serum into a dish, soaking it up in four-inch lengths of four-ply wool, and then inserting the wool under the skin of the animal's tail with a needle.

At first the wool had to be threaded through the eye of a needle, but one day when Charlie was a boy with his father on Strathmore they had all the animals ready for inoculation and then could not find the needle. Charlie's father put a small file on the grindstone and made a needle of his own. Unlike the one they had been using until then, it had a slot in the side instead of an eye and this made it easier to pick up the wool and saved a lot of time. Samuel Maunsell's emergency needle worked so well that he patented it, and for years the Maunsell needle, as it was called, was the best instrument for the job.

There were also calves coming on all the time, and this meant work like branding, ear-marking and castrating, which were done out on the run. Each beast had to be cut out from the mob and roped, which was slow, tedious work, and very hard on horses. Everything had to be done in the open; there were no yards except those at the homestead.

Pat Callaghan had refused to build yards out on the run because he said they only made things easy for the cattle duffers, who, when branding other men's calves, needed to work fast.

When the Boss took over he changed that and built yards wherever he thought they were needed. Callaghan was a man in his seventies and not able to get around the run as much as was necessary. The Boss, on the other hand, was always on the move and nobody knew where he might suddenly appear without warning. I remember the first time the musterers were going out, I said to him, "Where can I find you if I need you?"

"You won't find me," he said. "I never tell anyone where I'm going to muster."

"But why?"

"If I told anyone where I was going," he explained, "the next thing the mailman would know. He would tell them at every station he stopped at, and then the whole country would know where I was."

Tom Graham normally went with the musterers to

cook and look after the camp. "No doubt about Charlie being a silent man," he told me once. "We never know where he's going till we get there."

I soon learnt that you had to be careful what you said to some people out in the cattle country. There were several runs that were well known as duffing stations and every man had to look after his own. The Boss knew these parts, and was used to keeping his own counsel, and he was not going to change now, even for me.

There were also duffers who used to come from down Croydon way. The area round the lower part of the Gulf of Carpentaria—Normanton, Burketown, and those places—had been wild country from the early days when supplies for the north came in through the Gulf, and desperate characters drifted to those centres because they provided the best eating and drinking towns reasonably free from police interference. The Croydon gold-rush of the 1890s attracted more of them and gave rise to a duffing industry that still flourished. These men had their own outlets, and would run off any beast they could get their hands on. Most stations in our area were unfenced in those days, and there was not one fence all the way from Mount Mulgrave horse paddock to Cape York.

As well as building yards to make mustering easier, the Boss put in several cattle dips because this was tick country, and he also built a fence from the Mitchell River north as far as the mountain. As our boundary with Belle Vue station to the east was fenced, and the mountain stopped the cattle going any farther north, this gave us one very big, fenced-in fattening paddock for the steers.

What with one thing and another, the Boss spent so much time out on the run that the duffers did not have a chance on Mount Mulgrave while we were there.

Everything was new to me that first week on the station, and I managed to spend a lot of my time over at the yards where the men were getting the horses ready to go out. These yards consisted of a large mustering yard with a gate in from the bush, a drafting yard on the eastern side of it, and a cattle dip and killing yard. On the eastern side of the yards were large and small horse paddocks, and another paddock where the milking cows and killers were kept.

It was all arranged so the drafting yard had gates leading to the mustering yard, the dip, the killing yard, both horse paddocks and the cow paddock, so animals could be drafted wherever they were wanted. The drafting yard also had a gate on its northern side leading out to the bush to let out animals that were not wanted. Anything that went through that gate had an open run all the way from the Mitchell River to the tip of Cape York.

The mustering was so hard on horses that they always took several for each man and they never used the same animals on two musters running. The station kept from two hundred to three hundred horses, which normally ran in the big horse paddock and were used in rotation, being brought in to the small paddock and shod as needed. This meant that horses were spelling for several months, and when they were brought in they were often pretty wild.

In the small horse paddock were kept the horses that were being used, and two buggy horses, corn-fed, and always ready for any emergency. We grew our own corn on the banks of the river.

By the end of the week everything was ready for the men to leave, and a five-hundred-pound beast was killed for meat. That night it was fresh roast beef for all hands, and, as well as their usual rations, the blacks got the rib-bones, which they took over to their camp and roasted over a huge fire. Then they had a corroboree about "Killing the Bullock", every detail of the yarding and butchering of the beast being acted out in detail by painted blackfellows prancing in the light of their fire to the accompaniment of music made by the droning of didgeridoos, clicking of boomerangs knocked together, and the rhythmic clapping of the gins and piccaninnies.

There was an old man named Jimmy who was M.C.

at all their celebrations and he gave the tune which the others followed. We supplied him with tucker, which was taken to him by the other blacks, but we hardly ever saw him except at the corroborees, which we often attended. He preferred the old ways, generally ate the old foods, and spent a lot of his time in the bush.

Fresh meat would not keep for more than a day in that tropical climate, so all the beef that could not be cooked and eaten at once had to be salted. It was laid out in the fly-proof meat house on a bench raised at one end, coarse salt was rubbed into it, and the brine allowed to drain into a hogshead cask under the lower end of the bench. When the salting was complete, the meat was stored in the brine for use as needed.

Before it could be carried in the musterers' pack-bags, the salt meat had to be dried by being laid out on a sheet of iron and turned constantly. Then it was smoked by being hung in the closed kitchen all night. A big log would be put in the firebox, the covers taken off the top of the stove, and by morning the whole kitchen would be as hot as an oven, and the meat smoked as hard as a board. In the sultry summer months, or when there was nobody to look after it, the meat would not keep in the brine and all of it had to be smoked.

After having Sunday off, the men were ready to leave at daybreak on Monday morning. The horses had been yarded the previous night and everything left ready, and the musterers had breakfast by lantern light so as to get as far as they could before the heat of the day. It was so hot that horses and cattle could not be worked in the middle of the day, so the men made camp then and rested until the late afternoon when it began to get cooler.

The mustering party consisted of the Boss, Johnny Seibel as head stockman, Tom Graham as cook, Sandy Connors, half-caste, and three full-bloods—Maggie's husband, Dick, a very good stockman who had been born on the Palmer and worked with Callaghan since he was a boy,

Billy Charcoal, and Mitchell. Finlay, the fifteen-year-old half-caste lad, was in charge of the spare horses and pack-horses carrying ropes, swags, and tucker. The men had three camp horses each so the animals could be spelled regularly.

In addition to the dried salt beef, rations taken out mustering were mainly flour, cream of tartar and bicarbonate of soda for making dampers, tea, and sugar, all carried in little bags of unbleached calico tied up with tape and every bag a different size so the contents could be distinguished easily. There was always a good supply of tobacco and matches, and sometimes rice, curry powder, and treacle. They had billy-cans that were flat-sided so as to lie better against the horses' sides and all different sizes so they could be fitted one inside the other. A rifle and an axe were always carried, and Condy's crystals and Venice Turps in case of accidents. The Boss always wore a revolver in a holster on his belt.

I saw them off at the sliprails of the small horse paddock, and returned to see what I could do with some improvements I had decided to make about the house. Old Morisset had remained behind, and the Boss had told me I could call on two other old mates of Pat Callaghan's who had made the homestead their headquarters. One was an old fellow called Geordie Clifford, the other a man everybody called the Old Pole—everybody except the blacks, that is; they could not pronounce the letter P and to them he was "Ole Foal".

The house had two doors opening on the veranda facing the river, one from the bedroom, which was on the upstream side, and one from the dining-room. I moved the dining table and Austrian bent-wood chairs out of the dining-room onto this veranda, and from then on that was where we normally had our meals Another door from the dining-room opened on the veranda facing the kitchen on the downstream side.

There was also a door from the dining-room into the

bedroom, and each room had heavy wooden shutters that opened up and outward on the verandas. Dick McManus had sent up an iron bedstead and Paulina Fox had chosen all the blankets and linen. A couple of squatter's chairs completed the furniture.

All the outside doors opened inwards, and one of the first things I said to Mr Morisset was that I was going to have them changed to open outwards so I would have more room inside.

"You can't do that," he said. "In this country all doors must open inwards."

"Why must they?" I persisted.

"I'll show you."

He sprang to his feet, slammed the dining-room door shut and dropped into its sockets the heavy wooden bar that secured it. He did the same with the bedroom and back doors. Then he dropped each of the shutters and secured them all with the strong wooden latches that held them in place.

"See that?" he demanded. "All shut up and secure in less than half a minute."

I was staring at him in surprise. "I don't understand," I said.

He pointed to a series of round auger holes that had been bored in the shutters.

"See those? They're to fire a rifle through if the place is attacked by a mob of wild blacks. If those doors opened outwards you'd have to go outside to shut them, and as soon as you showed yourself you'd get a spear through you."

I had already heard of settlers being speared, but I think this practical demonstration of Morisset's did more than anything else to bring it home to me that I too was living in that sort of country, and the same thing could easily happen to me.

It also explained something the Boss had said before he left. We had talked about having two extra rooms built onto the side verandas of the house—one for him to use as an office so we would have more space inside, and one to use as a spare room. I had not liked the heavy wooden doors onto the veranda very much and said I would like to have them replaced by French doors.

"You can't interfere with the main part of the house," the Boss told me. "But if you can find any glass around the place you can have French doors on the veranda rooms." That was all he said. The Boss never told anybody more than he needed to.

I decided to get on with those two extra rooms and called in Geordie Gifford and the Old Pole to help. The latter had an old-fashioned pit-saw with which he provided any sawn timber that was needed about the place. Though quite an old man, he used to work the heavy saw by himself, standing on top of the pit with a big stone tied to the lower end of the blade. Those old pit-saws did their cutting on the downward stroke.

I got them to build the two new rooms on the corners of the veranda closest to the kitchen. We found some glass in the workshop—it was amazing what you could find in that shop—and they made two sets of French doors with it.

I used some of Paulina Fox's cretonne to make wardrobes—just a curtain hung from a stick across the corners of the rooms. "You want to keep those curtains a good foot clear of the floor," old Morisset advised. "If you bring them too low it's only a harbour for snakes."

I soon found the country was alive with venomous snakes of all kinds, from ten-foot taipans to three-foot death adders. There were also large rock pythons that grew to eighteen feet or more, but these were not venomous.

Dick McManus had told the Boss before he left Cairns that he would have to do something about all the old men Pat Callaghan had allowed to make their homes at Mount Mulgrave. They were independent characters and I saw very little of them. They all had their own horses, swags, and guns, and they would wander away shooting, fishing, or prospecting for gold when they felt like it, coming back to the station when it suited them.

When they were about the place I would tell Maggie to tell them to come up to the kitchen for dinner because I thought they needed a good hot meal. But they rarely did. They were tough old-timers, used to living on salt beef and damper, and they preferred to get a few rations and do a bit of cooking on their own fire down at the blacksmith's shop where some of them camped. They were quite comfortable there, and they wanted no luxuries except an occasional swig of rum.

When I was shown over the store I had seen two or three two-gallon demijohns of rum from which these men drew supplies as they needed them. Morisset had a five-gallon keg of his own, and a measuring stick so that after filling his bottle from the keg he could keep a check on what was left. They did not drink heavily, these old men, but they all liked to have a bottle of rum beside them at their camp so they could have a drink when they felt like it.

Most of these men had been born in the early days of the Palmer gold-rush and the thing that worried Dick McManus was that the time was coming when they would have to be looked after or taken into Chillagoe when they became ill. On a station nobody had time to spare for that sort of thing, and McManus wanted to get them closer to town where they would be able to get proper medical care when they needed it. Telling them they would have to go was going to come hard for the Boss. He was years younger than they were, but he had roughed it with a lot of them when he was on other stations in the north.

One of the jobs I had been left with was looking after the barrel of salt meat, but nobody had bothered to tell me what was to be done with it. The cook from Ceylon knew nothing of station life at all and old Maggie never thought to say anything about it. So I only found out when it was too late that every three days the meat should be taken out of the cask and put on the bench and drained, the brine boiled up, skimmed, and allowed to cool, and then brine and meat all put back in the cask. I just left the meat in the cask and it all went bad. All the help I got from Maggie when I discovered it was, "You no savvy bush, you only savvy town."

For the next three weeks until the men came back, we had to live on fish caught in the Mitchell by the gins. Everyone got tired of it, and old Morisset, who could easily have told me how to look after the meat, grumbled continually. He was very much the English gentleman, but he was well on in years at this time and often difficult to get along with.

He was very particular about his clothes and insisted on having a freshly washed and ironed shirt and pair of white moleskin trousers every day, which was more than even the Boss himself had. The job of washing and ironing them with old-fashioned flat-irons heated on top of the stove originally fell to Maggie, and one of her first complaints to me was an outraged protest, "Him make em wash trousers every day." The task eventually became mine because Morisset said Maggie did not do it properly.

Morisset's job on the station was supposed to be to milk the house cows, but he complained about having to go out and bring them in, and whenever Finlay was there he sent him to get them.

I was never able to understand how Morisset put up with the kind of aimless pottering about he did on the station. He told me he and his two brothers had been trained at the Royal Military Academy at Sandhurst, and he often spoke of his life as an officer of the Queensland Native Police Force. Station people I spoke to later told me they had known him in those days, when he had been a very handsome and dashing young man. They could not believe he had finished up as cow boy at Mount Mulgrave.

He had a wonderful library which was kept up to date by his sister, who had married Mr Philip Sellheim, the explorer, squatter, and mining warden. He also had a lot of the Morisset silver with the family crest on it, but he left this at the Imperial Hotel in the care of Paulina Fox. One treasure he kept with him was an old phonograph on which he used to play a collection of cylindrical wax records in the men's hut every night. The music used to come out of a big tin horn, which never ceased to fascinate the blacks.

One of the books Morisset lent me to read was Mrs Aeneas Gunn's *We of the Never Never*, but he first made me promise I would not read the end of it, which describes the death of Mrs Gunn's husband.

Though this was the dry season, one of the first things I did was to plant all the rose cuttings and other plants I had been given, and when Percy Parsons, the mailman, came I ordered seeds and seedlings. I had been told everything grew very quickly in the tropical Peninsula climate, and I hoped before long to have papaws, bananas, custard apples, mangoes, and dates. Maggie and one of the other gins had to carry water from the river in kerosene tins balanced on their heads, a job they hated.

I spent a lot of my spare time on the veranda sitting in the squatter's chair watching the crocodiles basking in the sun on the islands in the river, and the brolgas dancing on the banks.

My almost constant companion was three-year-old Robin, thoroughly spoilt because the blacks never punished their children, but amazingly quick and intelligent. He followed me everywhere and when I was reading or sewing used to squat on the floor beside me. The Boss had fixed the switch of a cow's tail to a stick, and with this Robin was supposed to keep the flies off me. But before we had been sitting down for long the switch would stop, and there would be Robin, sound asleep, curled up on the cool cement like a puppy.

In the afternoons I would go down to the river with the gins and piccaninnies, filing down the narrow track to the water with their washing—generally one old dress or a shirt—carried on their heads, their dilly-bags full of all sorts of odds and ends hanging down behind, pipes puffing in their mouths, matches stuck in their tangled hair, and all chattering away happily to each other. I followed behind, always mindful of a warning Tom Graham had given me: "Never let a blackfellow get behind you, even a gin; you don't know when he'll take it into his head to belt you over the skull."

But none of our people ever gave any trouble. The gins washed their clothes and hung them up on the bushes to dry while we all, myself included, swam and fished, someone always keeping an eye on me to see that I came to no harm.

About five o'clock in the afternoon we would all trail home—the house always seemed particularly lonely then— and I would look at the plants I had put in and get my dinner, which I ate alone. It was a tremendous adjustment I had to make after having grown up in a big family and being used to the gay social life of London. I used to think of my family a lot during those first evenings alone, and I wrote a lot of my letters at night.

I soon found there was more in the bedroom than bats, and some of the things that fell off the rafters after dark terrified me until I learnt how to handle them. There were snakes and goannas, centipedes, scorpions, spiders, and almost every kind of insect you could think of. The best plan, I found, was to pull the mosquito net down over the bed and tuck it in well while there was still daylight. Then I would put my books, writing paper, and sewing in under the net, light the hurricane lantern and put it on the table beside the bed, stand the loaded Winchester rifle against the wall—I would not have known how to aim it, let alone fire it in those days, but it made me feel safer—and I was ready for bed.

Old Maggie always camped by my front door when the Boss was away. After dark she would come over to the house with Robin, unroll her swag in the doorway, and sit there quietly smoking her pipe until I was ready to put out the hurricane lantern and go to sleep. Sometimes she would say, "What name you do now, Missus? You read em or you write em?" But she would never lie down until I blew out the light.

Even then it did not necessarily mean a night's sleep for either of us. Dingoes howled from the other side of the river and native cats, with big white spots and long-snouted faces, came in through the dining-room and fought under the bed.

I could never have done without that mosquito net. Goannas and snakes fell off the rafters onto it, and there were nights when there seemed to be bats everywhere. One night when I could not sleep Maggie and I killed forty-eight of them.

I always impressed on Maggie that she was never to touch the rifle because it was loaded and very dangerous. I succeeded so well that she became terrified of it, and when she came into the room in the morning to wash the concrete floor she would not go near it. There was a section of floor about two feet all round the Winchester that never got washed. She used to bring young Robin into the room and point to the rifle and say, "You no more touch em gun, him loaded."

As the day the Boss said he would be back got close, I spent hours watching for any sign of dust that would show the horses were coming. But the first I knew of them was Maggie's excited shouting, "Missus, Missus, him come now!"

I looked where she was pointing, but I could not see a thing—no dust, no speck of movement, nothing. But Maggie was right. Before long we saw the dust of the approaching horsemen. I was never able to make out how the gins always knew when the men were coming. I used to ask Maggie, and all she would ever say was, "You no more got em eye, you see nothing."

I was so excited I ran all the way out to the sliprails to meet them and tell Charlie how much I had missed him. We walked back to the house arm in arm, and I had so much to tell him about what had happened while he was away, and the mail from home and everything else, that I just talked on and on. I showed him all the things I had done around the house, and when we went and sat in the squatter's chairs on the veranda, I was still telling him about everything.

I was far too excited to notice that he did not seem to be paying any attention to what I was saying. He was always a quiet sort of man, particularly after he had been away for a while. It was probably because he was used to being alone so much. Anyway, I just talked on and on without stopping because there was so much to tell him.

After a while he got up without a word, went inside, picked up the gun, and walked away into the bush to get some peace and quiet.

CHAPTER SEVEN

❦❦❦

Christmas on the Mitchell

The men seemed to be out nearly all the time in those early days when the Boss was getting Mount Mulgrave shaped to his liking. If it was not mustering it was building yards or dips. He would come home, and he would no sooner have settled down, read the papers, and got used to me again, than it would be back to the old round of bringing in fresh horses, shoeing them, mending the harness, killing a beast for meat, salting it down, and away again.

The Boss had a lot of worries at this time. Fat cattle were bringing only from £2 to £3 each, and as well as having all the responsibility of getting the station in order and making it pay, he knew his mother's health was failing and he badly wanted to see her but could not get away. I had never heard of anyone working the way those men did, and there seemed to be no end of it. For me it seemed to be just day after day and week after week with nobody to talk to.

We had abandoned all efforts to make a station cook out of Sin Sin Yu, and the Boss had given him his cheque and put him on the track for Mungana with somebody who was passing through.

Morisset left us about the end of October, going out with Tom Graham when he took the wagon and six-horse team to Mungana to bring back the rations. I do not think he liked leaving Mount Mulgrave, but Dick McManus had found him a home at Kuranda where he would be better off, and closer to a hospital if he needed it.

A lot of the other old-timers also were disappearing. The Boss found places for some of them closer to civilization, but most refused to have any part of the offered help, rolled their swags, and walked away into the bush. They knew there would always be rations for them at Mount Mulgrave and they came in for them from time to time. I hardly ever saw them except when they were sick. Maggie or one of the other gins would come to me and say, "Old man, he come again, him sick."

I would go out and find one of the old fellows, generally half dead with the fever, lying on his blanket in the blacksmith's shop or under the buckboard. I would not know who he was and he would not want to talk, but he would have a small parcel with him containing all his worldly goods. He would hand it to me and say, "S'pose I die, send this to ——", naming some relation, if he had one, or maybe an old mate.

I would dose him up with quinine and feed him with good food, and more often than not he would get well—they were very tough, those old-timers—and he would take back the parcel, draw rations at the store, and walk away into the bush again.

I often used to say to the Boss after one of these men had gone, "I wonder how many nuggets of gold were in that parcel." A lot of those old men carried gold in their swags, and also a small pair of scales to weigh it out when they needed to buy something. Sometimes they would give a nugget to the mailman and ask him to bring something back for them on his next trip.

The musterers always kept an eye open for the tracks of these men. Sometimes when they followed a track they would find the man who made it dead under a tree. When that happened they buried him there and put a rail fence round the grave. More often than not there would be no name to put on it, but there would always be this little parcel containing the dead man's worldly possessions. One of the men would generally know whom it was supposed to go to, if not, the word would go round and Sergeant J. J. Magee at Maytown or somebody else would know. I must have seen dozens of those little parcels while I was in the north.

Approaching Christmas made me think more than ever of home and my family. At Ilford the snow would soon be on the ground; here on the Mitchell it was hot, muggy, and dusty. It would be the first Christmas I had ever spent with none of my family near. My two brothers who were in Australia were too far away for us to have Christmas together. Rupert, now married, was at Mitchell, about 1,500 miles away by rail and sea, and Tim, as far as I knew, was somewhere in the bush droving.

I wondered what they would be doing this Christmas. Would they be thinking of those white Christmases we had at home, when we would wake up and look through the frosty windows to see the front yard all white, and snow piled up against the house so we could not open the door without having it come tumbling down inside? We used to watch for the men who came round with shovels, and then bang on the windows and signal them to dig the snow away from the door and down the path to the gate.

At home at Ilford we always did things together and there was always somebody to talk to. Here, when the men were away, there was nobody. The black gins were not real company when you were lonely. Cheerful and happy as they were, I found that when I was feeling down their chatter only depressed me. They always seemed to be talking about people who had been killed. This thing about people dying seemed to have a special interest for them. They were quite cheerful about it all; it just seemed to be part of their lives. Everything was so different here.

One morning when the men were going away again it

all seemed too much for me. I saw the Boss off at the slip-rails and then I went back to the house and lay on the bed and cried. It was the first time I had given in.

The Boss must have thought I looked upset when I said good-bye to him, because he came back and found me crying. I was ashamed to have been caught, because I knew there was nothing he could do about it. The cattle had to be worked. But he comforted me and tried to explain things. Then he said if I could stick it out in the bush for ten years he would take me back to England to see my family again. Ten years seemed a long time then, but after that I had something to look forward to, and I never gave way to loneliness again.

Next time the Boss went out it was to build a stock-yard near the head of Sandy Creek, which joined the main stream below the Little Mitchell, and he asked me if I would like to go with them. There was nothing I wanted to do more. Though I had never ridden a horse in my life, I was ready to try, and I felt that camping out would be fun.

We packed the usual rations—dried salt beef, flour, cream of tartar and soda, tea, sugar, rice, curry powder, and treacle. They saddled me a quiet mare and we rode out about eighteen miles to the site of the new yards, made camp beside the creek, and had lunch. I was feeling stiff and sore from the ride, but glad to be with them. After lunch all the men and boys except Tom Graham went out with their axes to cut posts.

"If you want a swim," said the Boss as they were leaving, "go downstream."

To me, the water looked better farther up.

"Why downstream?" I asked.

"We don't want our drinking water stirred up."

At Tom Graham's suggestion, I collected dry grass ready for my bed that night, and then went for a swim. By the time I got back Tom had put up the tent for me, fixed up the camp and, before going off to help the others, made a damper and left it propped against a log to cool.

My swim had given me an appetite and the fresh, warm damper smelt so tempting that I cut off a crust, spread it with treacle, and ate it. Tom came back to get dinner ready and saw what I had done. Sadly he shook his head. "You should *never*," he said, "cut a hot damper."

At dinner that night the men, of course, all claimed I had completely ruined the texture of Tom's damper by cutting it hot, and made me feel I would never live down my mistake. But I was tired after my day in the open and I unrolled my swag early and prepared for bed.

"Where are the pillows?" I asked the Boss.

"Where are the what?" he asked in mock surprise.

"The pillows," I said.

"You use your saddle for a pillow."

He brought me my saddle and I did the best I could to make myself comfortable, but I could not. My grass bed was hard, and no matter how I arranged the saddle, my head wanted to roll off it.

Next morning I went out with the men to watch them felling trees for the fence. The day was hot and after a while I found a patch of shade and sat down in it. Next thing I knew was an anguished cry from Sandy Connors.

"Boss, look out! Missus sitting under tree."

I looked up and saw the tree swaying towards me, while the Boss, who had chopped it almost through, stood petrified. I scrambled to my feet and ran. The branches of the tree hit the ground and splintered just behind me.

For the next few days I managed to keep out of trouble, but when the Boss said he had to go back to the homestead for something, and asked if I would like to go home, I said yes, and I think everyone in the camp was relieved. I was certainly thankful that night to sit in a chair instead of on a log, and to sleep in a bed with a pillow.

The boys brought us two baby magpies, which we reared, and as they grew up they stayed around the house, followed us down to the river, to the yards, and everywhere we went. At night they camped on the iron rail at the head of the bed—always above the Boss's head, never mine. Sometimes we would try to trick them by putting the light out and changing places in the bed, but soon we would hear their little claws moving along the rail to get back above the Boss's head.

The magpies spent a lot of time on the tankstand looking round as though guarding their own private territory, and if any stranger crossed the river they would make such an awful din that we knew at once something was on.

One day they followed the Boss out to where he was yard-building. They were so tame that they got in the way and a log rolled on one and killed it. We were both very upset and the other bird was so lonely that the Boss thought it would be kinder to kill it.

It was about this time that Albert joined us. He was not a local Aboriginal but came originally from the Wide Bay district just north of Brisbane. He had been brought to Cooktown in the early days and employed there by Dr Khorteum (sometimes spelt Kortum) who dressed him in a white suit and trained him to open the door, show patients in, and drive the buggy when the doctor went his rounds.

After Dr Khorteum's death Albert somehow found his way to Maytown, and from there Sergeant Magee brought him to us. Albert was in his forties and right from the start I found him a blessing around the house. He was always spotlessly clean. We gave him a white suit and he looked after the washing and ironing and waited on the table inside as well as doing odd jobs about the homestead.

Another addition to our staff was Billy God-help-us, who came down from Frome with his wife, Kitty, and their two piccaninnies, Monty, a boy of about ten, and Charlotte, a girl of five.

Billy was the son of one of the Native Police troopers stationed at Frome, and the story went that he grew up so wild and spoilt that white men rarely referred to Billy without adding a good-humoured "God help us" to express their feelings about him. One day the priest came through and Billy was caught and brought before him for christening.

"What's your name?" demanded the Reverend Father.

Billy stared at the strange man in wide-eyed terror, and at last managed to blurt out, "Billy God-help-us." So Billy God-help-us he was christened, and Billy God-help-us he remained for the rest of his life.

He had worked for Pat Callaghan and was a fine, handsome man, more than six feet tall, well built, softly spoken, and always very kind to his family. His wife, Kitty, on the other hand, was a never-ending nuisance and caused more trouble among the gins with her gossip than all the others put together.

Billy worked mainly on the wagon, going with Tom Graham for rations, bringing in wood for the house and blacks' camp, and doing odd jobs about the place. When wire was needed for fencing, or cement for building cattle dips, it was Billy's job to cart them in from Mungana, and bring sand from the river. The cement in those days came from Germany in three-hundredweight casks and the Boss told me he had often seen Billy pick up a cask, get his knee under it, and lift it up onto the tailboard of the wagon on his own.

Rations came in twice a year, one loading before the wet season, and one after it. Their arrival that first November was a big occasion, and as the big wagon drew up at the store a shouting, excited throng of blacks gathered round it for the hand-out of lollies they had all come to expect.

Everyone helped to unload, but it took Albert and me days to arrange everything on the shelves. Six months' stores took up a lot of space and some things needed special attention. Potatoes and onions had to be put out on wire netting to keep them fresh, and one had always to be on the look-out for damaged packaging of things that might spoil.

The flour was full of weevils and the only way to get rid of them was to tip the whole four tons of it out on sheets of galvanized iron. The heat of the iron in the sun brought most of the weevils out, and then the gins and piccaninnies were given the job of scooping it up in saucepans and sieving it, first through a gauze meat-cover and then through small kitchen flour-sifters.

The bags, meanwhile, had been washed, dried, and sunned thoroughly inside and out, and the flour, less what had been lost in the cleaning process, was then rebagged. Four tons of flour took quite a long time to put through the kitchen sifters, and overnight the unsifted flour had to be covered with a large tent-fly to protect it.

The only way to keep flour through the wet season was to put half the consignment into a five-hundred-gallon ship's tank, stand a lighted candle on top of it, and quickly replace the cover and seal it with beeswax to make it airtight. The candle went out as soon as it had burnt all the air, and nothing could live in the tank until the seal was broken.

Additional items on that Christmas loading were: five gallons each of rum and whisky, one large case of Bulldog stout (for the Missus), one large case of Bass lager in one-pint bottles, one case of wine, one case each of tinned fruit and tinned crab, and three hams. There were also some laying hens, which we had asked Dick McManus to send to replace those his brother had eaten.

Jack Reid, of Gamboola Station, about thirty miles down the Mitchell, was an old mate of the Boss's, and when he had to go down to Gamboola just before Christmas I went along too. It was my first long ride in the north and I did not find it very comfortable. This was our midsummer, with the temperature well over a hundred degrees, and I made the mistake of wearing a black woollen divided riding skirt. Like most of the women in the north, I rode astride.

I knew it was going to be a dry trip and as a precaution I brought with me a supply of "quinine berries", a native berry about the size of a cherry. The blacks and some bush-men claimed that if you kept one of them in your mouth while riding you would not get thirsty. They were not meant to be eaten, just kept in the mouth.

It was a sweltering day. I sucked away at my quinine berry, but it had no effect at all. I was famished for water and nothing but water would do. But I dared not say so to the Boss. I knew he had trained himself to ride all day without a drink, and he expected everyone else to do the same. It was rarely enough that I was able to go out with the men, and I did not want to make a nuisance of myself within a few hours of leaving home.

Luckily for me young Finlay was as thirsty as I was and he knew the Mitchell was no more than a couple of miles away. We were following it down but keeping clear of it for the sake of the easier travelling provided by the open bush country. Closer to the river, the trees and undergrowth were thicker and in places almost impenetrable.

Finlay could not ask the Boss to turn in to the river so he could get a drink of water, but he thought that for the Missus it would be different. With the Boss riding out in front of us and Tom Graham behind, Finlay edged his horse up to mine and asked, "Missus, do you want a drink of water?"

I was so dry by then that I replied without thinking, "Yes, I do."

Finlay at once spurred his horse to catch up with the Boss. "Missus wants a drink of water, Boss," he said.

Without a word the Boss turned into the scrub, and we picked a track through it to the river. Never did a drink of water taste so good. Though none of them said so, I am sure everybody else thought the same. Finlay certainly did; he was a real water dog.

It was a different kind of country altogether close to the river—thick tropical jungle with long lagoons covered with water-lilies, and birds everywhere. In places, among the branches of the paper-barked tea-trees that lined the river, there were colonies of thousands of flying foxes, all sleeping and hanging head downwards with their leathery wings wrapped about them, red, furry heads like foxes' sticking out, and all holding hands together. In the late afternoon they would wake up and take flight in flocks so thick that they made a shadow over the setting sun.

On our way back to the open country I paid dearly for the delay I had unwittingly caused the party. The scrub was full of green tree ants, pale-green devils that made nests as big as footballs by fastening the leaves of trees together with a sort of webbing, and they stung like fire.

My horse brushed against one of these nests and within a moment the ants were all over both the horse and me. They got up my arms and down my neck and stung me all over. The horse reared and plunged, my skirt was torn against a dead tree, and I was nearly frantic from the stings before Finlay managed to grab the horse's bridle and lead us clear. By the time I had got rid of the last of the ants I was hotter and more uncomfortable than before I had been near the river.

After that we could not get to Gamboola quickly enough for me. When we arrived close to sundown I was tired, dusty, and sore, and the first thing I asked Mrs Reid for was a nice cool shower. By the time I was cleaned up and feeling myself again dinner was ready.

Old Tom Kilpatrick, of Southedge Station north of Mareeba, was there buying cattle, and he and Jack Reid found my experience with the tree ants very amusing. It put them in fine fettle for the meal and when Jack, who was carving, asked me would I like roast beef or tongue, old Kil came in quickly with, "Never offer a lady tongue."

We all had a very happy evening with Jack and Ann Reid and their two young daughters, Norma and Doreen, and when the Boss decided to go mustering with the men next day Ann asked me to stay with her for the fortnight until they came back.

We soon found something to do. Visitors and musterers coming into Gamboola homestead used to pull up at the harness shed and then had to walk right round to the other side of the house to get into the yard. A gate near the shed and a path and steps up to the veranda would have saved a lot of trouble, but though Mrs Reid had always wanted the job done, the station work always had to come first and Jack had never found time. I suggested we get the job done ourselves while the men were away.

Mrs Reid found an old gate with the hinges still on it, so we cut a piece out of the fence near the harness shed, put in two posts, and mounted the gate between them. We had the station gins clear a path across to the veranda and cover it with antbed while I got hold of the saw and cut a piece out of the veranda rail. The gins brought bricks from a heap of them that had never been used, and we stacked them up to make three steps to the veranda.

When the men came home at the end of the fortnight Ann and I were sitting in the deck-chairs waiting. They pulled up their horses at the harness shed, unsaddled them, walked in through the new gate, along the new path and up the new steps to the veranda, just as though all these things had been there for years. Not one word about the job we had done. Ann and I just looked at each other and laughed.

Ann Reid was reared on Mount Douglas Station, on the Belyando River in central Queensland, and though she had lived all her life in the bush she had preserved her complexion by always wearing three big veils, about a yard square, whenever she went out in the sun. I could never understand how she managed to see through them.

When the time came to return to Mount Mulgrave the Reids lent us one of those water-bags that hang round the horse's neck. I had had enough of relying on the blackfellows' quinine berries.

The day before Christmas the Boss killed a beast and the men all went out and shot ducks on the river, so we had plenty of fresh meat. We also had one of the hams, which I had cooked, and eggs from the laying hens Dick McManus had sent.

The men made a big plum-pudding mixture with

chopped suet, rich with plenty of dried fruit and rum, and we divided it into two puddings and boiled them in cloths for eight hours. I made a fruit salad from tinned fruit, and a custard. I cooled half the custard for the fruit salad by pouring it into a five-pound treacle tin, clamping the lid on tight, and putting it in a hole in the ground with ashes on top of it and filling the hole with water. The only thing we lacked in the food line was butter. The wet season was late that year and the milking cows had not been brought in.

Someone had sent me the recipe for hop beer, which I made by boiling two cups of hops and a quarter of a pound of ginger, straining this liquid into a four-gallon kerosene tin of water and adding two pounds of sugar. When it was quite cold I stirred in two bottles of yeast and bottled it, tying the corks down well to hold them when the yeast began to work. There were always plenty of empty bottles round a station homestead and we had ordered two dozen corks with the Christmas loading.

There was always an element of the unknown with the hop beer, because the yeast bottles, after being used for a while and becoming well seasoned, were very strong. Corks blew out, bottles burst, and drinkers sometimes found themselves with a brew that was stronger than they had bargained for. But everybody loved that beer, and, once I got properly into the way of it, I seemed to be making it everlastingly.

Most of the northern stations made their own drinks. The Boss told me that stations around Strathmore all made a very good effervescent drink from the wild rosella plant. The leaves were boiled up with sugar and the liquid was strained and bottled.

I learnt to make a fizzy drink powder by shaking together bicarbonate of soda, cream of tartar, icing sugar, Epsom-salt and a flavouring of lemon essence. A teaspoon of this stirred into a glass of water made a very refreshing drink in the hot weather.

When our fruit-trees came on I used to squeeze the

limes, strain the juice through muslin, and store it with a layer of olive oil on top. It would keep for months that way. Boiled up with sugar and bottled, it would last even longer.

We had with us as a guest that first Christmas Paulina Fox's nephew Jack, Mrs Hoare's eldest son, then a boy of thirteen on his school holidays and already planning his future career as an engineer. Billy God-help-us met him at Chillagoe with a spare horse and he rode the remaining seventy miles to Mount Mulgrave, camping out for one night at Nolan's Creek on the way. It would have been a notable ride even if the boy had been used to horses, but he only told us after he arrived that he had never been on a horse in his life until then. Within a few days he was out riding with the Boss to bring in the killer for Christmas dinner.

Every Sunday evening Jack would write to his mother. One night he was chewing his pen and said, "I don't know what I'm going to write about this week." Then a huge snake dropped from the rafters and landed right alongside him. The snake vanished in one direction and Jack in another. When he came back he had something to write about anyway.

Jack later played his own part in opening the north by becoming assistant to the chief engineer of the Queensland Government Railways. One of his brothers, Joe, became a solicitor, and the other, Mark, a judge of the Queensland Supreme Court.

After breakfast on Christmas Day all hands rolled up at the store. The boys all got new trousers and shirts, a pair of elastic-side boots, a fishing line, an assortment of fish-hooks, a new pipe and tobacco. The gins got a new dress each, a pipe, fishing line and hooks, and two two-shilling pieces. The last took a lot of collecting because very little cash was used in the outback, everything being paid by cheque. New clothes were tried on amid a great deal of horseplay, and everyone headed for the river.

There was more hilarity at dinner time, especially

when Maggie, her big enamel plate piled high with Christmas dinner, paused beside the gate of the paddock where the station stallion was running—we had to keep him near the house to prevent him from going wild. Maggie was having the time of her life and, pannikin waving in her free hand, was explaining to all and sundry, "No more want em tea, got plenty hop beer." The horse came over to investigate, saw his chance, and cleaned up everything on the plate—meat, vegetables, gravy and all.

A great roar of laughter from all the other blacks warned Maggie of what had happened. Her mouth fell open in dismay and she turned on the culprit in a fury, called him every name she could think of, and chased him right across the paddock, still screaming abuse, to the huge delight of everybody else. Only after we had refilled her plate did she quieten down and make off to the table, still muttering angrily, to eat her dinner before any further misfortune occurred.

❊❊➹➹

The Rising River

The Boss was fond of pointing out that the Peninsula suffered no droughts like those they got in the inland. The monsoons brought the rain regularly at the beginning of every year and our seasons were only two, the dry and the wet. Though they varied in intensity they were consistent, and everything that was done on the station had to be made to fit in with them.

January and February were the wettest months, then the rain slackened off and from the end of March until October there was hardly any at all.

Our busiest months were April, May and June, with fat cattle being mustered from good pastures and got off to the butchers. There was not a day to be lost because the country was drying out all the time. Creeks and gullies dwindled down to trickles, then to strings of waterholes, and at last dried out altogether. Water vanished from lagoons and by the end of June, all over the plains, dust began to rise wherever anything moved. Flies were everywhere. Cattle were beginning to lose condition.

The humidity was lower in the dry season, but there was no more than a few degrees of difference between summer and winter temperatures which, by October, reached 110 degrees Fahrenheit or more. I told the Boss once that the Peninsula was nine months summer and three months Hell.

Grass grown so rank that in places no more than the head of a man on horseback could be seen above it dried out. This was a time of fighting bushfires and keeping the cattle close to the Mitchell or the Palmer where there was permanent water. Parts of the plains dried out to near-desert in the dry. We used to put our fowls out on one of the islands in the river where there was always a picking of green, and take them off before the river rose in the wet.

By the end of October came the first scattered thunderstorms, bringing enough rain to fill a few waterholes and a fresh pick of grass to the parched plains. But they raised the humidity too, and the heat became almost unbearable. But this was no time to take it easy. The summer loading of stores had to be got in and dozens of last-minute jobs done before the wet turned the country into a bog that would make movement impossible. Once the wet set in it ruled our whole existence. The mailman came when his packhorses could get through, but often it was impossible. For weeks at a time isolation was complete.

In November and December the storms became more frequent. The river spread across its sandy bed and began to lap over the flats that bordered it. One by one the midstream islands disappeared under the water.

For the blacks, the rising river was Christmas. When the first floods brought roaring cascades of water over the rock bars above and below the homestead the boys would take the boat and drag it up-river past the rapids, and then all clamber aboard and come rushing downstream, cheering and shouting to the wildly excited gins and piccaninnies on the bank as they shot the rapids, swept past the homestead with their admiring audience running alongside, and on down to the foaming water of the lower cascades. Over and over again the whole performance was repeated.

Out in the bush the whole country was coming to life under the pouring rain. Deep cracks in the soil dissolved, lagoons filled and overflowed, creeks and gullies became foaming streams. When the sun shone briefly between storms you could see a misty layer of green beginning to spread over the bare soil. A day later it covered the ground, and in no time at all it was a lush growth that thickened day by day.

Huge flocks of all kinds of birds appeared overnight and crowded round the lagoons. Within days they seemed to be everywhere—black duck, big black-and-white magpie geese, cranes, teal, brolgas, and pelicans. The bush was alive with them.

Most of the Mitchell country was very flat, so the enormous amount of water that fell took a long time to get away. It filled the lagoons and shallow creeks and then over-flowed across the plains, flooding out all kinds of things that lived in the dust.

Before long the house was full of red-back spiders, scorpions and centipedes, and there seemed to be snakes in every corner and possible hiding-place. They swarmed into the store, the saddle room, the blacksmith's shop, the kitchen and the house itself. The Aborigines seemed to spend half their time killing them. I had never seen many of the things that invaded the place, and I got bitten twice, once by a scorpion, once by a red-back spider. Both bites felt like fire. The Boss cut them, sucked out the poisoned blood and doused the wounds with methylated spirits, which was our main antiseptic.

Other creatures the wet brought in were the guinea-fowl. Pat Callaghan had brought them to Mount Mulgrave in the early days to warn him when there were strange blacks about. They camped in the trees—with one eye open, it was said—and at the slightest unusual sound would set up a din that awakened the whole homestead.

By the time I arrived they had bred into a flock of nearly a hundred and were half wild. In the dry season we never saw them, but they came home in the wet for about three months, and every day they would lay their hard, brown-shelled eggs in the grass along the banks of the river. The gins brought in the eggs by the dozen. We ate them until we could eat no more. I made cakes and custards and omelets—anything at all that would use eggs—but no matter what we did with them, the time came when we were all, blacks included, so sick of eggs that we never wanted to see another guinea-hen.

By January the wet was at its height. It was not continuous rain, but was made up of very heavy storms which lasted for hours and then stopped, perhaps for a day or so, before being followed by more. I remember that first wet I was there how the Mitchell rose steadily. I used to watch the height of the floodwaters on the steep banks, and every day they were higher.

I remembered stories they told about the 1911 flood when Highbury homestead, about sixty miles downstream from us, three miles off the river and on nine-foot stumps, had been carried away, and the manager, Roly Bridge, and his family spent two weeks on a platform up in a tree. I had visions of the same thing happening at Mount Mulgrave, but the Boss was not concerned, even when the rain became continuous and thundered down as though it would never stop.

Then the Mitchell rose forty-five feet overnight. Next night it rose even more, and by morning had spilled over its banks. Water was lapping at the gate of the house.

That day the river was at least a quarter of a mile wide at the homestead, and from our vantage point on the veranda it was a glorious sight, though, to me at any rate, somewhat alarming.

Our boat, which had been securely moored to the river bank by a strong chain, was bobbing out in the middle of the flood, in constant danger of being smashed by tree-trunks and other debris brought down by the raging waters. The Boss, with two boys, managed to swim out to it during the day and, with both boys straining on the line to get some slack on the mooring chain, managed to unfasten it, haul it ashore, and tie it up at our gate. He said the homestead was in no danger because it was on a ridge and the floodwaters would break through lower ground and run away.

Next thing we knew, the Little Mitchell, which joined the main stream about a quarter of a mile below the homestead, was rising fast and bringing in an additional mass of water, which threatened to bank up the main stream and cover us.

It was all hands then to prepare a refuge. A roll of canvas was cut up to make big bags to put the food in, and all the old timber about the place was carted to the base of the highest tree ready to make a platform up in the branches to serve as a retreat if the river came higher. There was nowhere else to go. The homestead was on the highest ground within reach.

The water rose all that day until it just lapped the edge of our concrete veranda, then it stopped. The rains slackened, and slowly it began to recede. The worst of the wet was over.

By April the storms were gone, and then came the long drying out while the low country remained a bog. Nothing could be done out on the run and the men spent their time repairing and greasing the harness, fixing up the wagon, and doing some of the odd jobs that needed to be done around the homestead. They all had their minds on the big musters that would begin as soon as the ground was hard enough to move the sleek, fat cattle.

All around nature seemed to run riot to make up for the hard months of the dry. Grass grew rank and tangled, crowds of corellas and lorikeets flocked in to feed off the seed, cattle lazed in the shade too full to move. The blacks, who had their holidays in the wet, lived on the fat of the land, spearing ducks and geese along the river, wild pigs in the bush, and wading in the lagoons among the waterlilies to catch long-necked turtles with their bare hands.

Thick carpets of couch grass grew out over the lagoons

and floated on top of the water. Horses waded in to feed on it and lived so much in the water that the hair rotted off their tails, leaving only stumps, and leeches clung to their sides bloated with blood like huge grapes.

These leeches caused cankers which had to be cut out, especially when they affected valuable horses like good breeding mares. The boys would throw the animals and tie them, and then one boy would hold each leg and another would sit on the head. The Boss would have a very sharp knife, a fish-hook fastened to a length of string, and a bucket of Condy's crystals. He would start by putting the hook into the canker—some of them were very big—and then he would cut round it until he had the whole thing out. Then he would take the hot searing irons from the fire and cauterize right round the wound before finally putting on Stockholm tar to keep away the flies.

The poor mares would groan all the time the operation was going on, but they generally got well. Albert, who was very gentle and good with animals, had the job of hand-feeding and watering them until they recovered.

As the ground began to dry out, rice grass, which grew out in the swampy country, was cut with a scythe just as the seed formed, loaded on a wagon, and stacked on a frame about two feet above the ground. Then it was sprinkled with a layer of coarse salt and covered with a thatch roof until it was needed to supplement the maize that was fed to the working horses during the dry.

The Boss had been telling me since I arrived that when the river fell after the wet and uncovered the fertile river flats we should plough them up and plant our vegetable garden. By June they were dry enough and work on them began. The maize was put in first because it would be needed for the horses. We normally grew from ten to fifteen tons of it.

After the maize was in we planted the sweet potatoes and all the other vegetables. We had written away to the Department of Agriculture and Stock for seeds and I was surprised at the selection they sent us. We had about thirty different kinds of sweet potatoes alone, all different shapes, colours, and sizes, as well as English potatoes, pumpkins, onions, silver beet, turnips, carrots, parsnips—in fact, almost everything you could think of.

While they were planting I spent most of my time down at the river planning it all. The only things that worried me were the mosquitoes. The floods had left pools of stagnant water lying all along the river bank and the mosquitoes bred in their millions and attacked us in swarms, biting savagely, with their heads down to bury their stings in the flesh and their tails sticking straight up in the air. There was nobody to tell us that these were the characteristics of the *Anopheles* mosquito, carrier of malaria, or Gulf fever as it was generally called in the north.

Mount Mulgrave was always a bad place for the fever, probably because the homestead was right on the river bank. At other places, such as the Walsh, they never had it at all. A strange thing about it was that some people lived in the Peninsula all their lives and never had a trace of it; others died of it in their first year there. At Mount Mulgrave it followed a pattern. As soon as the Mitchell started to go down we got the mosquitoes and the mosquitoes brought the fever. I eventually learnt to keep away from the river immediately after the wet, but that first season I did not know, and all the rest of that year I had recurring bouts of fever.

As well as the vegetable patch, we were beginning to get quite a nice garden going round the house. Most of the cuttings I had been given had struck and were growing. My original granadilla cutting grew so well that I was eventually able to take about a dozen more cuttings from it. The Boss and the boys built a long path to the back gate. We planted the granadillas along it and when they grew he put up a trellis of wire netting to make a covered walk of it. The local native bees ignored the granadilla flowers, so every morning I spent an hour or more cross-pollinating them by hand with a small camel-hair brush. The result was worth the trouble and before long we were picking granadillas by the clothes-basket full.

Mrs Evans's mango seedlings from Wrotham Park flourished, and we also had bananas, papaws, custard apples, and citrus-trees coming on. Everything grew very quickly in that climate.

I also had a lot of ornamental trees and shrubs. To keep Kitty out of mischief I sent her out to the dump to collect empty bottles and set them into the ground to make borders for three large flower beds about five feet across, which I planted with annuals and frangipani and other plants. Kitty did not like the gardening job at all and she protested loud and long: "Too much work, too much work."

One of the frangipani trees had been given to the Boss as a cutting by Mrs Magee at Maytown, and he had put it in his saddle and forgotten all about it. It did not come to light until three months later when he told one of the boys to grease the saddle. In spite of its rough beginning it grew into a beautiful tree.

On the western end of the veranda facing the river the Boss built a fernery by putting in posts ten feet apart and stretching wire netting over the top of them. Flower-pots were hollow logs with pieces of tin nailed over the bottom, and we hung these from the cross pieces. Mrs Evans sent me cuttings of her beautiful dark-red climbing begonia and this soon covered the whole fernery. After the windmill was put in I used to hose the fernery down to cool it before dinner.

The windmill was one of the first things the Boss had ordered after he took over. Once it was installed down by the river, and a good high thousand-gallon tank put up, we had all the water we could use during the dry season. Before every wet we had to dismantle both windmill and pump and store them safely above flood level until the river went down again. During the wet we relied on our rain-water tanks.

The Boss wanted Dick McManus to send another windmill for the middle of the run so the stock would not have to be mustered onto the rivers all the time, but McManus said there was no money for that, and those dry-season musters remained a regular thing at Mount Mulgrave.

Most of the ferns and orchids in my fernery came from the original Mount Mulgrave, the limestone peak from which the station took its name. It was a beautiful mountain about ten miles to the north of the homestead and halfway between the Mitchell and Palmer rivers. Its slopes were riddled with caves in which the blacks had left their paintings, and over its rocks cascaded clear streams fringed with all kinds of ferns, ground orchids, and other tropical plants. It was in this limestone country that the Cooktown orchids grew at their best, and before long my fernery was a mass of their mauve blooms.

If ever the Boss ran short of rations when out working with the cattle he would send one of the boys—generally Dick so he could see his family—with a note of what he wanted scratched with the point of his knife on the lid of a Bell and Black's wax-match tin: "Mail, flour, tea, sugar." If they were in country where there were ferns or orchids growing he would fill the pack-bags with them and scratch "ferns" on the tin so I would ask for them and make sure the boy had not thrown them away as useless.

At first I used to ask the boy where the musterers were, but all I could ever get out of him would be, "Might be one mile, might be two mile." Most likely they would be several miles away at the time. The blacks had no idea of giving distance in miles.

When I knew the bush better I learnt to ask, "What time you bin leave em camp?" Then I would at least be able to work out from his time of arrival about how far away the men were.

The musterers generally took no luxuries with them, but when I filled the bags I would often put in a loaf or two of fresh bread and some butter if we had any at the time. The butter would be running by the time it reached their camp, but I always put it in a tin and it could be hardened by being put in a creek for a while.

Before long I had the homestead surrounded by a beautiful tropical garden filled with fast-growing fruit-trees and flowering frangipani and bougainvillea, and the fernery a mass of ferns, orchids and begonias. With the vegetable garden also flourishing, I was beginning to feel we were on the way to living quite well at Mount Mulgrave.

CHAPTER NINE

❦❧

The Myall Midwife

Soon after I arrived at Mount Mulgrave Arthur White and his wife Maud took over the Walsh Telegraph Office from the Emersons, and on 24th April 1913 their lineman rode up with a letter from Arthur asking me to come over at once, because Maud's second baby was coming prematurely.

Luckily the Boss was at home; he straight away sent a boy out to bring in horses and we were able to leave soon after. It was only my second long ride in the bush and I had an unpleasant trip. Although it was April, the northern autumn felt like the middle of summer to me, and the horse I had, a big chestnut hack called Cooktown, seemed to realize my inexperience and would not do a thing for me. No matter how much I urged him on, we kept lagging behind.

"He's the best walker on the station," said the Boss when I complained. Perhaps he was, but he was not going to walk his best for me. "Here," said the Boss at last, "I'll lend you one of my spurs."

I buckled on the spur, Cooktown still hung stubbornly back, and I gave him a dig with it. He bounded away like a rocket. I had not enough experience to hold him and it was all I could do to stay on his back.

The Boss stopped us at last by galloping ahead and

cutting him off. I did not use the spur after that and Cook-town, realizing he had me bluffed, made his own pace. By the time we reached the Walsh Office it was dark.

Arthur White, after sending the lineman for us, had himself ridden all night to Blackdown Station and brought back an old gin called Fanny who delivered most of the piccaninnies in that part of the country. Arthur was terribly worried and was reading up in a medical book what should be done. Fanny was getting ready to bunk down beside Maud's bed. There was time for me to have a shower and clean-up and a rest on a stretcher before the baby came. Throughout the whole thing the calmest of us all was Maud herself.

I remember I was in her bedroom with old Fanny, and Arthur White was outside the door with the medical book reading out what we should do. But what was actually happening seemed quite different from what he was reading, and while I was trying to understand it all old Fanny just ignored us both and went ahead with whatever it was the blacks normally did. Arthur kept calling out, "Don't take any notice of that old black fool; this is what the book says."

The baby girl arrived in the middle of it all, and I remember calling out to Arthur, "How long does it say I've got to cut the cord?"

There was a pause while he looked for the place in the book, and then he read it out, but it was nothing like what Fanny was doing. I tried to get him to describe it more clearly. He was nearly frantic with worry.

"Never mind old Fanny," he yelled. "Just do what the book says."

I was watching Fanny and I thought, "She's brought more piccaninnies into the world than Arthur White has ever seen." So I let her go ahead without interfering and everything was all right.

Baby Iris was born on 25th April. She was a seven-months baby, and so tiny I could have put her in the pint jug. I did not know if I should bathe her or what I should do. I finished up putting the little mite on a towel on the bed and sponging her. Then I dried her and gave her to her mother.

Maud was only twenty-one at the time, and I never knew anyone so placid and understanding. The Boss had to go back to Mount Mulgrave, but I stayed on for a fortnight. Iris was a lovely little girl. She is a grandmother now, and in 1972, almost exactly fifty-nine years after she was born, she and her mother came to see me in Brisbane to talk over those early days on the Mitchell.

I learnt a lot about life in an outback telegraph office during that fortnight I stayed with the Whites. Maud was the telegraphist and that meant she could never leave the place. Twice a day there was a special call on the office Morse which meant the line was open for her to send any telegrams or messages. I got to know the signal so I could tell her they were calling.

Maud had been born and bred in the bush on Maryland Station, on the border of Queensland and New South Wales near Stanthorpe, and was a very good judge of horses. When the Boss arrived at the end of a fortnight to take me home he had once again brought Cooktown for me to ride. He himself had a mare named Biddy. Maud came out to see us off, took one look at Cooktown, and told me, "You've got the wrong horse." At her suggestion the Boss and I swapped horses and I saw at once what she meant. Biddy was what they called an ambler, with an easy gait that made her much more comfortable for a woman to ride than a horse like Cooktown. She gave me no trouble at all on the ride home, and became my favourite mount from then on.

Among the blacks the birth of a baby hardly interrupted a woman's daily routine. Shortly before Maud White's baby arrived Kitty had her second daughter. She was born during the night, and in the morning I went over to the camp to see her. She was a dear little thing, as all the black babies were, and as I held her Kitty asked me to name her.

"You make em name for her, Missus."

"Call em Josie," I said.

"All right," said Kitty. "Now I bin give em alonga you."

The blacks often gave children away like that, especially if they had one or two others already. I did not want a little piccaninny to look after at that time, so I shook my head.

"You keep em now." Then, seeing Kitty's look of disappointment, I added, "Later on I take em."

That same morning Kitty was up at the house looking for work as though nothing had happened. I sent her back to the camp for a week and told her to look after the baby.

As things turned out, I did "take em Josie" in the end. About nine years later when my own son, Ron, was born and I needed someone to look after him, I said to Kitty, "I take em Josie now?"

"All right, Missus," she agreed happily, "you take em." So Josie, by then a girl of nine, came to live at the house, and she remained with us until Ron started school.

Maud White needed a young gin to help her in the house, and she asked Sergeant Magee next time he was in the northern part of the Peninsula to see if he could bring her one back.

Native girls needed to be trained young if they were to be useful about the house, and it was always best to get someone from a distant tribe if possible, because she was less likely to be wanting to spend all her time down at the blacks' camp, and was more likely to be trustworthy if there was trouble with the local blacks. Each tribe in the Peninsula had its own territory covering about a hundred miles of country and each spoke a different dialect. Except on special occasions, members of different tribes did not go beyond their own borders.

When Magee next came through Mount Mulgrave on

his way back to the Walsh, he had two young gins with him. He had got a little girl of about eleven from the Coleman River tribe, about 120 miles or so to the north, and her elder sister, a girl of about fifteen, had been so upset about it that she had run behind Magee's horse all the way down from the Coleman. Some of the country was quite rough, and by the time she got to Mount Mulgrave her feet were so cut and sore that she could not go any farther. Magee said he would leave her with me while he took the younger one on to Mrs White. When he returned the girl he had left did not want to go home, so I said she could stay with me. I called her Mary.

The Coleman blacks were still wild cannibals at that time, and Mary had had her two top front teeth knocked out as part of her initiation into womanhood. She could not speak a word of English and knew nothing at all about station life. I told Albert that if he could teach her to speak English and make herself useful about the place, he could have her for his wife. "You teach em speak English, you can have em Mary."

Albert could not marry any of the local gins because he did not belong to the district, and Mary would not have been able to marry into the Mitchell tribe either. Among the blacks neither party to a marriage had any say in it; everything was arranged by the old men in accordance with strict rules of relationship.

All the Peninsula blacks had been cannibals originally, though, according to some of the old-timers, different tribes seemed to have different rules about it. Men killed in warfare were generally eaten by their own people, but in the gold-rush days a lot of white men and Chinese were killed and eaten by the blacks, apparently just for food.

One day a Chinaman came to the station looking for a job and I said to Mary, "Mary, you bin eat em Chinaman?"

She shook her head emphatically. "No more. Him too salty. White man more better."

Most of the old-timers I talked to used to say the

The Evans family at Ilford in England. Middle row, left to right: Fred, mother, father, Evelyn. Back row: Ida, Rupert, Hugh. Front row: Ralph, Basil. Aubrey, generally known as Tim, was away at sea when the photograph was taken.

Evelyn Maunsell on her wedding day at Cairns on 21st July 1912.

The honeymoon buckboard. Charlie Maunsell in the driver's seat, and Billy Evans, manager of Wrotham Park Station.

Charlie beside Mrs Ferguson's Abbott buggy during the honeymoon trip to Mount Mulgrave.

On her first Sunday at Mount Mulgrave Evelyn goes boating on the Mitchell River with her husband. The homestead is at the top left-hand corner of the picture.

Tom Graham and Billy God-help-us bring the wagon over the Mitchell River crossing with the Christmas rations.

Evelyn in the shade of the lime which was the only fruit tree growing at Mount Mulgrave when she arrived. Behind her is the galvanised-iron shower room, through the floor of which Dick McManus fell.

Evelyn on the Mount Mulgrave homestead veranda with Charlotte and Robin.

Evelyn and Charlie in their two-year-old Mount Mulgrave garden. The granadilla trellis is on the left.

The musterers return to the homestead. Charlie Maunsell is on the right.

A mob of Mount Mulgrave cattle on the bank of the Mitchell River.

Aboriginal stockman, Dick, handles a freshly broken horse at Mount
Mulgrave.

Albert in his waiting-on-table suit.

Mary soon after she arrived at Mount
Mulgrave from her home on the Coleman River.

Police Sergeant John James Magee, of Maytown.

Evelyn and Bridget on the bank of the Little Mitchell River.

Charlie with two of his race horses, Gay Lass (left) and Mayflower, the brumby mare.

The girls of the Palmer River at the time of the 1916 race meeting. The eldest girl, on the left, is Gracie Gordon.

The four-in-hand in the bog. Left to right: Tim Evans, Charlie Maunsell, Blue Whittaker.

Overnight camp beside the flooded Walsh River. Left to right: Bridget, Blue Whittaker, Charlie Maunsell, Garnet Evans, Evelyn Maunsell (almost obscured).

Rafting the buckboard across the Walsh River. Left to right: Finlay, Charlie Maunsell, Blue Whittaker, Bricky, Garnet Evans.

Mrs Jack O'Brien and Con O'Brien with some of the Mount Mulgrave staff. Left, back: Kitty with piccaninny Josie. Right, back: Albert and Maggie. Front, left to right: Monty, Robin, Charlotte, Mary.

Coming down the straight at the Walsh River races.

Sergeant Magee drops his hat to start the gins' race at the Walsh River races. Friday Butcher urges them on.

Some of the Aboriginal staff at Wrotham Park. Left to right: Finlay, Bricky, Charlie Inkerman, Scotty, Monty (in front), Palmer, Gilbert.

The old shed which was the first Wrotham Park homestead. All the iron for the roof was brought up by packhorse.

Posing for their pictures in front of Wrotham Park homestead, left to right: Frank Simpson of Lochnagar Station with his daughter in front of him. Duncan McLean of Koolatah Station with Edie Rafter in front of him. Evelyn Maunsell, Charlie Maunsell and Alice Rafter. All three men were more than six feet tall.

cannibal blacks preferred Chinese to whites because the whites were too salty. Maybe things were different up on the Coleman, or perhaps Mary was just trying to impress me.

Albert and Mary got along well together and she was very happy with us. The Boss built them a house of their own not far from ours. Albert taught her some English, how to set the table, and do all the housework like sweeping, dusting, cleaning the floors and washing. He did the ironing and waited at table. Maggie looked after the kitchen.

In spite of all Albert's patient teaching, there were one or two things Mary could never master. I remember one wet when the Mitchell came up very high and we moved the dining table off the veranda facing the river onto the northern veranda. In its original position Mary had learnt to set the table perfectly, but moving it confused her completely. She just walked unhappily all round it with the knives and forks in her hand and could not work out where to put them. Albert had to come and do it for her.

Once while the musterers were away Maggie got sick. I could not make out what was wrong with her, but I told her not to come up to the house to work, and I cooked her the kind of food you would cook for any invalid—beef tea, poultry, custard and so on—and took it down to her at the camp. She ate it to please me, but she showed no sign of improving, and by the time the musterers, including her husband, Dick, returned she was no better. Dick apparently summed up the situation and he asked the Boss if he could go walkabout and take Maggie and Robin with him. They all set off and we did not see a sign of them again for about a month.

Then one day Maggie appeared at the kitchen. She had apparently just put on an old dress, but I could see that underneath it her usually plump figure had wasted away almost to skin and bone. I have never seen a black gin look so dreadful. She pulled aside the dress to show me big weals on her body and on her arms where the skin had been cut with something sharp and ashes rubbed into the fresh wounds. Her head was all bandaged up in bark so I could not see what had been done to it.

In spite of her starved appearance and terrible wounds Maggie pronounced herself cured. "Me bin all right now, Missus. Me work all right. Him bin let em bad blood out. No more sick now."

Dick had apparently taken her back to their original tribe in the bush somewhere and the witch-doctor had gone to work on her.

I cleaned her up as well as I could and got her into fresh clothes. I heard later that down at the camp that night Dick cooked her a large goanna which she devoured on her own. From then on she never looked back and was soon her old self again, except for the large weals on her body and arms. They would remain for the rest of her life. The blacks always claimed that goanna fat had special medicinal properties. From what I saw of it, anybody who could eat it deserved to get well.

The blacks were pleasant company if you treated them properly, and ours were all very happy and contented. The Boss had grown up among them and knew how to handle them, and they all liked and respected him. I learnt a great deal about Aboriginal customs during the days I swam and fished in the Mitchell with them.

In their natural state neither men nor women seemed to wear very much in the way of clothes, and they did not bother a great deal about shelter at night, except that they generally lit a few small fires round them and hollowed out a spot in the ground to lie in. During the wet they made small platforms to sleep on, and roofed them with sheets of bark bent in a half-circle. They built smoke fires to keep away the mosquitoes.

They had their stone tomahawks, barb-pointed spears, spear-throwers or woomeras, and boomerangs, and they wove bark nets to catch smaller game. Once they came in contact with the whites they were quick to make use of any scraps of metal they could get, and they soon acquired a few white men's tools like tomahawks.

Before they got used to station tucker almost any kind of meat was regarded as food, even crocodile. Our blacks had all the salt beef and vegetables they could eat and they supplemented their diet by hunting and fishing. Wild pigs were favourite marks for their spears, and the boys often caught young pigs and brought them in to the homestead for fattening. Lizards, goannas, and big rock pythons, which looked like chicken when cooked, were all good food to the blacks. Cooking was generally done by wrapping the meat in green leaves and covering it with hot ashes in the camp-fire.

The rainbow had a special significance for the blacks; it was connected in their minds with a mythical being called the Rainbow Snake, and this had something to do with their creation myth. All over the Peninsula there are caves decorated with drawings of this snake, also men and animals and various kinds of designs. There were a lot of these painted caves on Mount Mulgrave, and more in the hills near Mungana.

They had different kinds of corroborees for different occasions, some apparently very ancient, others more recent. One of them was a most realistic re-enactment of a prospector with his dish washing for gold beside a stream.

One night while the Boss and I were watching a corroboree at our blacks' camp, a strange blackfellow came into the firelight all on his own. He wore nothing but a sort of lap-lap, he carried a spear and his hair was all waxed out. None of our boys knew him. They let him go into the circle beside the fire and do his dance, and then he just walked away into the bush. I think our people were afraid of him because he was a myall.

Our half-civilized blacks were inveterate gamblers. When the winter loading came in about June all the blacks received an issue of blankets, but they rarely kept them for long, particularly if the nights were warm at the time. Cattle buyers would come in with their own blacks, there would be a corroboree down at the camp that night, and as well as the traditional Aboriginal entertainments there would be a lot of gambling and the blankets changed hands in the process. The first cool night that followed, there would be a line-up of blacks at the store complaining, "No more blanket, too much cold." We would have to make good the gambling losses of all concerned.

Sometimes I went hunting with our gins in the bush and I found they used all kinds of foods that white people never heard about. They collected the seeds of different kinds of grasses and made a sort of flour of them. There were certain kinds of berries and a type of wild grape they were very fond of. They ate lily roots from the lagoons, and even made something like bread out of the nuts of the pandanus palm.

They also collected two different kinds of red and black beans, which they called gidea, the larger ones growing on trees, the smaller on vines. They pierced and threaded these to make beads and also pressed them into soft beeswax or gum to decorate woomeras and the like.

The gins taught me to make fire by spinning a fire-stick between my palms in a small hole cut in another stick, which was held firmly on the ground with one foot. The idea was to have a small heap of very dry grass, and as the sparks appeared, push the grass on them with the free foot, still keeping up the spinning until there was enough smouldering grass to pick up carefully and gently blow into a flame.

The piccaninnies, until they were old enough to be initiated, were taught by their mothers and were generally very quick to learn. Maggie's young Robin, though only getting on for four by this time, was already a good tracker. After the men had gone mustering Robin would walk out to the horse paddock with me and show me everything that had happened.

"See here, Missus," he would say, pointing to the ground, "Billy Charcoal, he bin catch em horse here."

Then, a little farther on, "He bin canter now." Then again, "He gallop here. He bin see em big mob horses now. He bin take em yard."

I could never make out what he saw on the ground to tell him all that. He could even tell the difference between each man's tracks.

His knowledge of nature was amazing. He would show me the tracks of different kinds of ants and tell me where they were going and what sort of nest they had. He showed me how to follow native bees to their nest. Once he brought me the whole contents of a bower-bird's playground, and among all the bits of coloured stone, shells, and broken glass was a pair of steel-rimmed spectacles which had been lost long before by one of Pat Callaghan's old-timers.

As soon as our vegetable garden was going well we used to boil up a four-gallon kerosene tin of sweet potatoes every day for the house and the blacks' camp, and it became Maggie's job to dig them. Robin used to find the biggest ones and bring them to me, and I had to measure them alongside him to see if they were as big as he was. There were none quite as big as that, but it made him happy to be told, "My word, that big feller, bigger'n you." Or else I would say, "My word, you bin beat em this time", and that pleased him most of all.

I taught the gins how to make popcorn by roasting corn in a hot pan, and I gave them sugar to coat it with. Piccaninnies, gins, and boys alike all loved it.

Once young Robin got so completely out of hand that Maggie appealed to me, "You make em savvy, Missus."

I said to Robin, "You no good feller, you bad feller", and locked him up in the corrugated-iron store. After a while I thought he was so quiet that I had better make sure he was all right. Opening the door very gently, I was confronted by two big, happy black eyes and a wide, white-toothed grin. Robin had climbed on a case to reach one of the food shelves and had spent his punishment gorging himself on dried apricots and raisins.

Robin always came to the sliprails with me to meet Charlie when the musterers came home, and the Boss, who was as fond of children as I was, used to get off his horse and lift Robin up into the saddle. It was a treat Robin always looked forward to, but one day he fell off and put his teeth through his bottom lip. The Boss carried him home and we bathed his lip and gave him a handful of sweets, which soon stopped his crying, but by then Maggie had arrived in a fury. "No more put him on horse like that," she protested. That night Robin was the centre of a big corroboree that went on into the early hours of the morning.

By this time I was expecting my first baby and we were looking for a good cook who would relieve me of the cooking. As it turned out we were lucky.

There were still some Chinese scratching around the Palmer River goldfields and nearly all the gold they found went straight to old Ah Look, the storekeeper at Palmerville, to buy opium, possession of which was illegal. Sergeant Magee made an occasional raid on the opium smokers, and when he had rounded up a batch of them he often sent for the Boss, who was a J.P., to hear the cases.

One of these calls came about this time and one of three Chinese charged with having opium illegally was none other than old Ah Quay, Samuel Maunsell's Strathmore cook, by now ancient, wrinkled, and ugly as sin, too stiff in the joints to work in the garden, but a past master in the arts of station cooking and everlastingly cheerful. Charlie fined him £15 for having opium, paid the fine himself, mounted Ah Quay on one of the spare horses, and brought him back to Mount Mulgrave to cut out his debt.

Ah Quay was an excellent cook and, if anything, he looked after us too well, always making sure that the Boss and I had everything of the best, and the rest of the staff what was left over. When cooking the tongue of a beast, which he did very well, he would send the whole of it in to the Boss and me. He had no idea of dividing it up so the men could have their share of it. If he made a large tart or a pie, the whole of it would always be served to us.

As well as a constantly increasing supply of vegetables, we had more eggs than we could use. The cows had come in during the wet, so we had plenty of milk, cream, and butter, which I made myself.

We were kept constantly supplied with fish from a trap the Boss had built just upstream from the homestead and baited with a shin-bone. There were also freshwater crayfish, which Ah Quay made into an appetizing dish, a plentiful supply of duck from the lagoons, an occasional plain turkey, and pork from wild pigs which the boys caught young and fattened up for killing. There were two kinds of wild pigs in the north, the big, long-snouted, high-shouldered wild pigs said to be descended from animals brought to the north by Captain Cook in 1770 and therefore generally known as "Captain Cookers", and smaller ones whose ancestors had run wild more recently.

But in spite of all the good fresh food they had to choose from, everyone except me seemed to have a constant hankering for the everlasting salt beef, dried out hard and then soaked overnight to make it soft enough to cook. Fortunately Ah Quay, with the help of a mysterious supply of Chinese herbs he obtained from his countrymen, could make even salt-beef rissoles appetizing.

Next time the Boss went out mustering he told Ah Quay to look after me, an arrangement that gave me some confidence because Ah Quay, in spite of his fearsome appearance, was very loyal to the Boss and thoroughly reliable.

One thing I overlooked was that Chinese do most of their cutting up with a heavy steel chopper and they often work during the night. One morning I was awakened at 2 a.m. by Ah Quay, chopper in hand, putting his head through the shutter of my bedroom window and, with a terrible grimace which no doubt was meant for a reassuring smile, inquiring, "You all right, Missus?"

Ah Quay was very happy at Mount Mulgrave, but by the time he came to us he was a very old man and one day he told the Boss he would like to return to China. The Boss lent him the £8 for his fare home as a deck passenger and Ah Quay left for Mungana with the wagon when it went out. He sent back the money the Boss had lent him, but we never saw him again.

Some time later three Chinese arrived at the station looking for work, and the Boss engaged the most promising looking of the three, a man named Won Kow. But Won Kow as a cook was one cow of a nuisance; the men used to say he was worse than six cows, and in due course he also got his fare home to China. The Boss never hesitated to lend them the money for their fare. The Chinese were scrupulously honest and it was always repaid.

CHAPTER TEN

❧❧❧

Gulf Fever

I picked up the Gulf fever just after the river subsided in 1913 when I was down on the flats all the time getting the vegetable garden started. I had several bouts of it during the year, but managed to keep it at bay with quinine.

That November was sweltering hot, the early storms were heavier than usual and the rivers were rising. Working the cattle had become difficult, but there was still a lot of work to be done to bring Mount Mulgrave up to the standards that would suit the Boss and, threatening though the weather was, the packhorses were loaded once again and the men went out on the last long trip of the year. The Boss expected to be gone about four weeks, which would get him back in plenty of time for Christmas.

He was barely gone when the malaria hit me. For days I just lay in bed, sometimes burning with fever, then shaking with chills, hardly able to move. The unlined galvanized-iron bedroom was like an oven in the daytime so I got Albert to bring a stretcher from the men's quarters and put it on the veranda near the kitchen for me. (This I have already described in my first chapter.) Those were special stretchers made of laced strips of greenhide that let the air circulate, and were cooler to sleep on than anything else.

After I had the miscarriage, I did everything I could think of, but I knew nothing about proper treatment and within a few days I was so weak I could not move. For days on end I was too ill to get off the bed. For nearly two weeks I had nothing to eat at all.

At times I knew there was someone talking to me, but I could not pull myself together enough to answer. Once I asked Maggie to bring me a cup of tea and she brought me the billy off the stove, all black with soot, thrust it at me and said, "Here y'are, Missus." Faithful old Albert hovered close by all the time, but there was nothing he could do.

Percy Parsons had given up the mail-run and Herb Doyle, formerly of Frome, had taken over. The blacks probably told him I was sick, but he could not have realized how sick I really was. Maud White, at the Walsh, did not know about me. She told me later, "Even if I had known, I couldn't have come." She had her work cut out with the Telegraph Office, which could not be left, and looking after little Iris and another young child. Iris was still too small to be left behind or taken out twenty-five miles in the wet.

Just lying there in the terrible heat day after day and not being able to move, I was sure I was going to die and I could not stop thinking about what would happen when I did.

It was then that I said, "Albert, s'pose I die, you dig a hole and put me in it, and cover me up, and tell Boss I bin lose em piccaninny."

Albert kept saying, "You no more die, Missus. You no more die." If it had come to the point I do not know if he would have buried me or not. He was frightened and would not face the possibility.

I made Maggie bring me the whole pile of clean sheets and I picked out the strongest of them so they could carry me in it if I died. I could not do much to help them get it under me, but they managed somehow.

Next day Albert came to me and said, "Missus, you give me gun." The Boss had always impressed on me never to give any of the black boys a gun in any circumstances, but I was too sick to care and I told Albert to take it. He picked it up and walked out of the house with it without saying what he was going to do. He was away so long that I began to worry about what might have happened.

He came back at last driving a cow and calf and carrying a brolga's egg he had found and two ducks he had shot. He milked the cow and made a baked custard with the egg. It was so strong I could hardly eat it, but I did my best because he had been so kind and I did not want to hurt his feelings. It was a big thing for Albert to take the gun against the Boss's orders and go out alone looking for food for me. He was a stranger to that part of the country and the local tribal blacks were out to kill him if they got a chance.

Then he steamed the two ducks. He cooked them well enough, but spoilt them by putting in curry to flavour them. I managed to eat a little of it and I began to feel a bit better after that.

By the time the Boss was due home I had decided not to tell him how sick I had really been. I heard him coming and tried to get up out of bed to meet him, but it was no good, I fell down in front of him and he got an even worse shock than he would have done if I had stayed in bed. He picked me up, carried me into the bedroom, and laid me on the bed. I was just skin and bone, and must have been hardly any weight at all.

The stretcher on the veranda was in full view of the men coming to the store, and he left me inside while he went out and stripped off all the dirty bedding and dumped it in a tub in the laundry and covered it, and told Albert to take the stretcher back to the men's quarters.

After that was done he came back to the bedroom with a bucket of warm water from the kitchen and gave me the first wash I had had for three weeks. He got clean sheets and a nightgown, propped me up with four clean pillows, combed and plaited my hair, which was a terrible, tangled mess, and gave me a good shot of overproof rum.

Then he said he would be away for an hour or so because he was going out with Sandy Connors to bring in a killer and a couple of milking cows. I did not mind. The fresh, clean sheets felt wonderful, it was good to have him home again, and I began to feel better than I had done for weeks.

When he came back he said I still had the fever and gave me another dose of raw quinine. Then he sat on the bed, took off his leggings, spurs, and revolver belt, went out and had a shower and came back and sat on the bed holding my hand until I went to sleep.

When I woke up he was lying beside me wide awake. "What's the matter?" I asked.

"I haven't been asleep all night; I never thought you'd see it through," he told me.

But I felt all right now he was there to look after me. He went out that morning and killed the beast he had brought in and made me beef tea from a fresh shin-bone. There was plenty of fresh milk, too, and Charlie looked after me better than a nurse could have. It was a thing I always marvelled at about the Boss. He had lived a hard life from when he was a small boy, and had seen men die in the bush many times, but in a case of sickness he was the most gentle and considerate man I ever knew.

From the time he returned I began to feel better. After four days I managed to walk to the shower, which was not far from the bedroom, though Charlie had to help me back. It was wonderful to feel clean again and to have someone near.

The wet-season storms were becoming more frequent and there was still work to be done out on the run, but the Boss let it wait and found things to do around the house. When it was not raining he would take a mattress out and put it under a shady tree and carry me to it so he could keep an eye on me while he worked. He used to encourage me to walk, and joke about my thinness. "Two pounds five shillings for just skin and bone," he would say. He never could forget that money he had to pay for the special marriage licence.

But in spite of all he could do for me, Christmas came and went and we could both see that I was not going to get better without being treated by a doctor. By then it was the middle of the wet, the rivers were up and the black-soil plains a bog in which a buckboard would sink to the axles. If I could only get out to the railhead at Mungana I would be all right. The Boss asked me if I thought I could sit on a horse to make the trip. It was about sixty-five miles and normally took two days by buckboard.

I told him I would give it a try. I had been telling him all the time that I was not as sick as I really was, and I could not give up the bluff now, even though I did not know how I should manage to ride. When he was sending the boys out for the horses I remembered Maud White's advice and told him, "Be sure to tell them to bring in Biddy."

The horses were swum across the Mitchell and hobbled to hold them there while saddles, pack-saddles, swags, and myself were ferried over in the boat.

As though Charlie did not have worries enough with me, we were just starting when we met the lineman from the Walsh Telegraph Office bringing a wire from my brother Rupert to say that Charlie's mother, who had been bedridden for months, and whom he was planning to visit as soon as he could manage to get away from the station, had taken a bad stroke and would not recognize him even if he did come.

I shall never forget that nightmare ride to Mungana to catch the train to Cairns. The heat was dreadful and I was even weaker than I had thought. The trip took us six days, but luckily there was no heavy rain. I was so weak I was only just conscious a lot of the time. Charlie kept bringing his horse up to mine, putting his arm round me and saying, "Just try to do another mile or two, then we can get into camp early."

But every few miles I had to get off Biddy and sit under a shady tree to rest. Sometimes Charlie would give me a nip of brandy, and before the trip was over I had drunk about a bottle of it.

At the Walsh crossing there was a boat for use when the river was too deep to be forded. It was on the other side when we arrived, so Charlie swam the horses across and then came back in the boat to get me and the gear. Then came the business of climbing onto the horse all over again. Every mile we did seemed to me like the last I would ever do, and how I made it to Mungana I shall never know. I have often heard it said that the Lord especially looks after the people in the bush.

The Boss had to go straight back to Mount Mulgrave, so he phoned Dick McManus to meet me at Cairns and left me in the train in the care of Darby Riordan, the guard. I think I slept for most of the trip, and Dick McManus met me and took me to the Imperial Hotel.

Next morning Dr Kerwin, whose surgery was just across the street, said I must have a constitution of iron to have gone through what I had, and sent me to hospital for two weeks. At the end of a fortnight he let me go back to the hotel, but said nothing about when I could return to Mount Mulgrave.

I was feeling so much better by then that I told Dick McManus to book me a seat on the train at the end of the week and wire the Boss that I was coming. It meant that Arthur White's lineman would have another twenty-five-mile ride across country to deliver the wire, but I felt the Boss had enough worries on his mind about his mother without my adding to them.

The Boss met me at Mungana with a hired buckboard and driver who took us as far as the Walsh, which we crossed by boat. Finlay was waiting on the other side for us with the Mount Mulgrave buckboard, which the Boss had managed to get through to there, and when he saw us coming he had put the billy on for a cup of tea.

Nearly all the way back to Mount Mulgrave we seemed to be ploughing through sticky black mud, but it was nothing at all to that terrible ride out. What Dr Kerwin said when he found I had gone home without his permission I never did find out.

※←※

Bush Surgery

Dick McManus and Paulina Fox were married about April 1914 and came to stay with us at Mount Mulgrave during their honeymoon. They were comfortable enough in my spare room with the home-made French doors, but Dick was fond of the comforts of town and not used to bush makeshifts. He was a heavily built man and had not been with us long before he crashed through our shower-room floor and gashed his leg very badly. He was less fit than a bushman would have been and the leg refused to heal and became infected.

The Boss was a great believer in hot water and Condy's crystals, so he made a special bath by cutting the bottom out of a kerosene tin and soldering it onto the top of another one. This gave enough depth to soak the whole of Dick's leg at once, a treatment he submitted to only with a great deal of complaint. The pain, he said, was excruciating.

No doubt it was, but the word was a new one to Tom Graham, who had received all his schooling in the bush, and Tom found it amusing.

"Hey, Charlie," he asked the Boss one day, "what's this word 'excruciating' mean?" The Boss told him, and Tom chuckled over it for weeks. "Excruciating," he used to say to himself. "It's excruciating."

The leg showed no sign of healing and Dick and Paulina had to cut their honeymoon short and return to Cairns, where the doctor told them that but for the Boss's hot-water treatment Dick probably would have lost his leg.

Dick had suggested to the Boss that it would be a good idea to leave a white man at the homestead with me when he went out mustering in future, so next time the men went away Tom Graham remained behind to keep an eye on me. He and the Boss had been mates since the early days.

Tom, then about forty, had been born on the Palmer River during the gold-rush, and after the field petered out he and a few of his mates had worked some of the old mines in the Maytown area. They had been beaten by the water that seeped into the underground workings, but Tom still maintained there was a lot of gold to be got from those reefs if only the water could be pumped out for long enough to mine them.

Except for one brief trip to Cooktown several years before I knew him, Tom had never left the Palmer and Mitchell country in his life, and his ideas on the rest of the world were rather vague. After Charlie had gone down to Nockatunga Tom wanted to write and give him all the station news and ask how he was faring in the Channel Country. He remembered the Boss had gone to Sydney first to visit his mother, so a letter duly arrived addressed: "Maunsell, Nockatunga, via Sydney".

Tom was a first-rate bushman and handy at all station jobs, though by the Boss's standards a bit too ready to say, "That's near enough." I have never forgotten watching him and the Boss working together when I was out on their yard-building trip to Sandy Creek. As the Boss saw things, a post had to go into the ground two feet six inches, and that was it. But if Tom happened to hit a rock there seemed no point to him in smashing through it. "Ah, that'll do for our time," he would protest.

Left to look after me, Tom used to busy himself about the homestead all day, and after dinner at night he would bring a hurricane lantern and sit on the veranda and smoke his pipe and entertain me with his droll yarns about the early days, in which he always figured as the fool, though he was far from being that in actual fact.

He was, however, very superstitious. He would never go near Pat Callaghan's grave after sundown, and as soon as it began to get dark he would hurriedly pick up his lantern and make off for the men's quarters, leaving Maggie, young Robin, and me to settle down for the night alone.

"I wouldn't sleep in this house, not if you gave me a thousand pounds," he used to tell us. "Pat Callaghan shot himself over there and"—nodding in the opposite direction—"that's where the Chinaman cut his throat."

After he had left several nights with this announcement, I found myself jumping at shadows. When the Boss came back I learnt that the Chinaman, for some reason unknown, had actually cut his throat down on the bank of the river. But I had heard enough about him anyway. Next time the men were getting ready to go out I said to the Boss, "You can take Tom with you, he scares the life out of me."

One evening the Boss said there was a family camped down at the Mitchell crossing and he was going to see who they were. They turned out to be Mr and Mrs Willie Stewart, their daughter and two sons. Willie was a son of J. B. Stewart, who had originally taken up Drumduff Station on the Palmer, and a brother of Jimmy, who was then running it.

The Boss invited them to camp at the homestead and they stayed with us for a week. They were overlanding from Gordonvale, just south of Cairns, to take up Starcke Station, on the Starcke River, about fifty miles north of Cooktown. In a straight line it was about 130 miles from Mount Mulgrave, but the intervening country was some of the roughest in the State.

Starcke had been taken up years before but abandoned soon after. There was no house on it, but the Stewarts thought there was some sort of a shed. They planned to get any building material they needed from Cooktown, which since the gold-rush days had shrunk so rapidly that more than half its buildings were empty and deserted, fast falling down from the ravages of cyclones and the raids of settlers needing timber.

The Stewarts were travelling with a big wagonette, half covered by a tarpaulin, and jammed full of clothing, bedding, utensils, and almost everything that could be of use to a family heading out into new country. All the family rode their own horses, they drove cattle and goats, and carried several large crates of fowls.

While they were with us the Boss let them keep their cattle in a corner of the horse paddock and tail them during the day. They all did their washing and a lot of cooking for the road, and we sent them on their way with all the fresh vegetables and meat they could use.

The Stewart boys had gone fishing and left the fishing line hung up on the veranda to dry by taking it from one nail to another along the railing. After they had moved out and our men had gone mustering, I picked up the line, not knowing the hook was still there, and got it deeply embedded in my first finger. I could not get it out, and for two nights I slept with my hand held up in the air to ease the throbbing pain.

By Sunday the finger was swollen and poisoned and so sore that something had to be done. When Herb Doyle, the mailman, arrived I had a knife all cleaned and sharpened and I asked him to cut the hook out for me. He had a look, turned very pale, and said, "I couldn't do it, Missus, you'll have to wait till the Boss gets back."

The Boss would be out for a fortnight, so after Herb had left on Monday I got the knife and told Albert to hold my finger as hard as he could to make it numb. Then I started to cut the hook out myself. Albert gritted his teeth and turned his head away. "I no more can look, Missus," he said.

I had to cut almost to the bone to get that hook out. Then I poured methylated spirit over it to clean it and bandaged it up.

Herb was another of those men who had grown up in the bush and he always knew more about what station people were doing than anybody else in the Peninsula. He told me once that his father, John Doyle, was the man who discovered the Barron Falls. Later on I went and saw old John Doyle, who was then living in a ten-foot-square galvanized-iron shed on the bank of a creek outside Mareeba.

Doyle would have been well over seventy by then, and he told me he had been born at Goulburn in New South Wales, and had known the bushrangers Ben Hall, Johnny Gilbert, and Frank Gardiner. He came to Queensland for the gold-rushes at the end of the 1860s, did a lot of exploration work, and found the falls in October 1876 while looking for a practicable track between the Hodgkinson goldfield and the coast. He died in 1933, aged ninety-one.

We were always having accidents on the station and there was a lot of bush doctoring to be done, especially when horses were being broken in. When there was no mustering to be done the boys would bring in brumbies from the ranges and pick out some of the best of them for breaking. When the day came to ride them the gins would come to me in great excitement. "Missus, come along yards; they ride em today." The gate would be opened and the horses would come thundering out, bucking and rooting and twisting everywhere, some riders staying on, some falling off, boys cheering, gins screaming with laughter. These were the real buckjumping shows and broken limbs were fairly common.

There were also some falls while mustering. Treatment of a broken limb out on the run was simple but effective. The Boss would set the fracture on the spot, cover it up with tea-tree bark, and strap it up tight with stirrup leathers or swag straps. I never knew one of his bush doctoring jobs that did not heal properly.

For lesser injuries he was a great believer in Venice Turps, a mixture of resin and turpentine of about the appearance and consistency of treacle. It was wonderful for drawing splinters and poisonous thorns, which were plentiful enough in the bush, and was one of our main stand-bys. Dick McManus, after his own unfortunate experience, sent us up a fully equipped medicine chest, but the Boss had little time for such newfangled contraptions. He preferred to rely on a few old and well-tried remedies.

I myself had come back from hospital well stocked up with Dr Koah's Fever Mixture. It was better than raw quinine as a preventative for fever and was a good tonic as well. Dr Koah was wonderful with fever cases and he did so much for the north in the early days that the people of Cairns put up a monument to him.

I also made use of some of the old herbalist remedies I had picked up from my Grandpa Evans at home in England. One of these was made by pouring methylated spirit over a bunch of parsley and covering it until the parsley was white and the methylated spirit green, and then straining the liquid and bottling it. Rubbed into the skin it was good for rheumatism, and I used it regularly on Charlie's back, which gave him a lot of trouble as a result of his breaking a hip while working at Lyndhurst Station before we were married.

One of the most anxious days I had at Mount Mulgrave began one morning when the Boss and Dick had gone out early to bring in a killer from where the beasts were running two or three miles away. The first I knew of anything wrong was when I saw the Boss's horse, still saddled and with reins dangling, pull up at the sliprails. There was no sign of either the Boss or Dick.

It turned out that something had started the cattle running, and when the Boss had galloped round to stop them his horse put his foot in a hole, fell, and rolled on him. The Boss was unconscious and Dick spent the rest of the morning riding backwards and forwards to a waterhole about a mile away, bringing back a hatful of water at a time, and pouring it over the Boss's head.

Charlie came to about midday to be greeted by Dick's relieved grin and, "My word, Boss, you bin asleep a long time."

On another occasion the Boss and Dick had been fighting bushfires all day and by afternoon were close to collapse. Luckily for the Boss, Dick finally drew the line. "No more," he said. "Drink em water, Boss."

He led the way to the nearest waterhole and the two of them waded in, flopped down and lay there, keeping their heads just clear of the muddy water and soaking it up through their skins.

They arrived home about dark, almost too exhausted to move. I put a camp bed on the veranda between the house and the kitchen where it was coolest, made the Boss lie on it, covered him with wet towels, and put up the mosquito net. He lay there for three days while I kept the towels wet all the time. He was lucky to recover.

The most amazing piece of bush doctoring of all occurred a few years after this when Dr Tunstan, of Chillagoe, a French Canadian, suffered an acute attack of appendicitis. There was no other doctor within miles and he had to operate on himself.

With the help of the matron at the Chillagoe hospital, he managed to remove the appendix at last, but what with the pain of the operation and the difficulty of seeing what he was doing, he almost disembowelled himself in the process. When he came to put his insides back where they belonged neither he nor the matron could manage it.

At last they gave up the job as impossible. The matron bound a sheet round the doctor's stomach to hold everything in place as well as possible and, with several helpers, managed to get him onto a railway pump car. With Dr Tunstan propped up on the only seat, the matron standing alongside to steady him, and a railway porter pumping for dear life, they covered the hundred miles or so to Mareeba in record time.

The doctor survived the journey, a colleague put the displaced parts back where they belonged and sewed him up, and he made a good recovery. Dr Tunstan was an unusual man in a lot of ways, but after that he had a right to be.

CHAPTER TWELVE

❊❊❊

The Barbed Spear

The fact that I was not speared the first time wild blacks raided Mount Mulgrave homestead was probably due mainly to the loyalty of our station blacks. It was nothing spectacular, that raid, no war yells and spears flying round the way some people seem to expect. It all happened so quietly that I did not know it was on at first, and it was only about half-way through that I realized how close both Albert and I were to being killed.

There were always wild blacks roaming round on the outer fringes of the run. Cattle were speared, and I knew the Boss, like other cattle-men, was hard on any raiders he caught. The myalls generally kept clear of homesteads, but station people were still being speared in the north in those days, and there were always a few groups of blacks who were prepared to raid a homestead store if the opportunity offered and put a spear through anybody who got in their way. They were generally led by "cheeky fellers" who had had some contact with white people.

Old Morisset and Tom Graham had said enough to make me realize that both Albert and I would be in danger if myalls ever came to the homestead when the Boss was away. If any of them had any accounts to settle with him, I could easily be the one to pay.

Albert was in even more danger because he was an outsider from the south who, in their opinion, should have known better than to be trespassing on their territory and, further, to have married a gin he had no right to. The fact that Mary was very happy with the arrangement had nothing to do with it.

Maggie and the other blacks at the homestead camp were in a peculiar position. They were all Mitchell River people like the wild blacks. They all met and hunted together when they went on walkabout and their children were all initiated at the same ceremonies. If myalls came to the homestead to raid our stores our people could not afford to offend them. They would all talk together and be quite friendly. But at the same time our blacks were loyal to us and would look after us in any way they could.

At the time of the raid I was alone at the homestead with Maggie, Kitty, Mary and Albert. Young Robin was away somewhere with the other piccaninnies, and the other gins were over at the camp as usual. I had noticed all the morning that the gins did not seem to have their minds on their work. They just seemed to wander about the place as though they were filling in time waiting for something to happen. I learnt later that this was a sure sign there were strange blacks about.

Then I noticed these strange blacks coming in through the sliprails. There were ten or a dozen of them, all naked except for a sort of little lap-lap thing they wore, and they had boomerangs, spears and woomeras.

Kitty and Mary were outside. Albert must have been in one of the other rooms. Maggie saw me looking and came and stood at the door with me.

"Them wild blackfeller," she said, "but you be all right."

There was nothing menacing about the men. Some of our people were talking to them and I noticed they were walking towards the store. The next I saw of them they were coming towards the house. I looked at Maggie.

"You be all right, Missus," she said. Then she walked out towards the back gate to meet the myalls.

I do not know where Albert had been until then, but suddenly he was alongside me and he was shaking with terror.

"Missus, Missus," he gasped, "wild blackfellow come along now with spears. They kill us all."

That was the first hint I had that we were in any real danger. I remembered what old Morisset had said about bolting the door and shutters and I had turned to Albert to tell him to help me do it when I heard the voice of one of the myalls talking to Maggie. A lot of those myalls had learnt a few words of English from the station blacks.

"Where Missus?" he demanded.

"'E longa river," Maggie replied.

I paused in the act of closing the door. If I shut and bolted it now they would know I was inside. If I kept quiet, perhaps they would believe Maggie and go away.

"Keep quiet," I whispered to Albert, and I beckoned him to follow me into the bedroom. In there we would be less likely to be seen if the myalls looked into the house. Albert picked up the shotgun and followed me.

I sat on the bed. Outside I could hear the myalls jabbering away to Maggie in their own language, and then the one I had heard before spoke again.

"Where Albert?"

"'E longa river," said Maggie.

There was a movement beside me and I saw that Albert, gun and all, had slid under the bed and was crouching there like a dog in a thunderstorm.

The myalls had reached the veranda. Quietly I slid down beside Albert. The bed had an old quilt that hung nearly to the floor. From under the edge of it I could see across the concrete to the bottom of the curtain hanging in the doorway between the dining-room and the bedroom.

Albert's teeth were chattering. He was clutching the shotgun to him with one hand, and in the other he had a box of cartridges. I heard some of the myalls come into the living-room.

"Where Missus? Where Albert?" came the same voice again.

"'E longa river."

Hardly breathing, Albert and I lay still. I was looking across the floor to the bottom of the curtain. I saw the barbed point of a spear come through at the side of the curtain and push it aside as if to let the owner peer into the bedroom. Just beyond I could see a bare black foot.

For what seemed an age I waited, my eyes fixed on that savagely barbed spear-point. At last it was withdrawn and the curtain fell back.

We heard them leaving then, but we remained where we were until a long time later, it seemed, when we heard Maggie's voice. "All right now, Missus, him gone now."

The myalls had taken all they could carry from the store and they got clear away with the lot. When the Boss returned he tried to follow them, but rain had fallen in the meantime and washed out their tracks.

Next time there was trouble I realized earlier that there was something wrong, and I was better prepared for it.

At this time we had working for us a black boy named Charlie Inkerman. We knew nothing about him, but he had come to us almost starving and said he would work for his tucker, so we gave him a job. It was not a wise thing to do, but he seemed all right at the time. As it turned out he was in with a couple of wild blacks from the north and trouble developed just after the Boss and the men had gone out on a muster.

The first thing I noticed was that the gins would not do any work. They just wanted to roam around the place as they had done before. I knew by then that this meant there were strange blacks about and something suspicious was going on. I was ready to slam and bolt the doors, but saw no sign of strangers.

That night the kitchen was raided and a lot of food stolen. It was no good asking the gins about it because of their divided loyalty to me and to their own people.

Later that morning I was in the garden. It was Charlie Inkerman's job to water the garden, but he was not doing anything. I told him to water the garden. He made no attempt to do it, just looked at me.

"You water garden," I told him again.

"No more!" he exclaimed. Then, when I stood my ground, he added more quietly, "You want to look out, Missus."

The implied threat was obvious. He knew as well as I did that the musterers had left twenty-four hours earlier and should be miles away by now, and I was alone at the homestead. He just stood staring at me.

Then, out of the corner of my eye, I saw across the yard to the sliprails and—the last thing I had expected—there was the Boss coming through. Something had made him come back. I turned and walked into the house. Inkerman, from where he stood, could not see the sliprails, and as soon as I was out of his sight I ran through the house, out the back and across to the yards.

No time to tell the Boss how glad I was to see him. "Charlie Inkerman's round by the river," I gasped. "He won't water the garden. He told me I'd better look out."

The Boss said not a word, just hitched up his horse and came striding over to the house. "The kitchen was raided last night, too," I went on, half running to keep up with him.

Straight into the office for the handcuffs went the Boss, then round to the front of the house. Inkerman saw him coming and made a dash for it, but he was too late. The Boss grabbed him, snapped on the handcuffs and held him tight.

"Where two feller?" the Boss demanded.

Inkerman hung his head sulkily but remained silent. The Boss clouted him across the head and repeated the question. "Where two feller?"

Still no answer. The Boss turned to me.

"There are two strange blacks on the station," he said. "We saw their tracks and came straight back. I'm going out after them."

We had a stockman named Hughie Louden working for us at the time, and the Boss, Louden and Albert got fresh horses and rode out after the two myalls. Inkerman still refused to talk and they took him with them, handcuffed and running behind Louden's horse at the end of a rope. Albert went along to look after the horses in case of trouble. If the myalls were local men Albert would be more reliable than the other station blacks, and he would not stray too far from the Boss for fear of getting a spear between his own ribs. The Boss was armed with a revolver— he never moved far from the station without it—and Louden had a Winchester rifle.

They got on the two myalls' tracks, followed them out for about ten miles, and surprised them making camp on the Little Mitchell. As luck would have it, the blacks had put down their spears and walked away from them to collect wood for a fire.

The Boss rode between them and their spears, and when they ran away into the bush he grabbed the spears, broke them, and threw them into the fire before riding off in pursuit. He and the others caught the men, took their dilly-bags, which contained food and other articles stolen from the homestead kitchen, gave both of them a hiding, and told them never to show their faces on the run again.

They brought Inkerman back to the homestead, still running behind Louden's horse. There was not much cheek left in him by the time they got back and his bare feet were cut and bruised from running over the rough country.

The Boss wrote a letter to Sergeant Magee at Maytown telling him what had happened and sent it by one of our own boys. We had to hold Inkerman chained up in a tin shed until Magee arrived. He was a small man, and when they put the handcuffs on him they were too big to hold him securely, so the Boss tied them with wire to make them smaller and twisted the wire tight on the cuffs with a pair of pliers.

By daylight Inkerman was gone. He must have worked on that tightly twisted wire all night with his teeth until he got it free and was able to slip his hands out of the cuffs. They went after him and brought him back and put leg-irons on him then.

All the time Inkerman was a prisoner in the shed poor old Albert looked after him, taking him all his meals and bathing his cut feet in warm water and disinfectant. Inkerman was a Palmer River man and he would have killed Albert if he had got the chance.

We had to keep him at the station for two weeks until Magee came to pick him up, and all that time the Boss stayed at home. He never said anything to me about what he was thinking and it was only later on that I realized how worried he was about me.

Every night we would go to bed in our own bedroom and then, when everything was quiet, the Boss, saying never a word about why he was doing it, would get up and arrange two pillows in the bed to make it look as if we were still there. Then he would take me by the hand and take me round to the spare room to sleep. Before it was daylight he would wake me and we would get up and make the bed and tidy the spare room so it would look as if no one had been there, and then creep back to our own room. We would wait there in bed until Mary brought our morning cup of tea.

This went on every night. "You're mad," I used to tell the Boss. "What are you doing all this for?" But he never told me a thing.

When Magee came at last I said to him, "What's wrong with the Boss? He keeps taking me to sleep in one bedroom and about eleven o'clock when everything is quiet he takes me into the other, and when it's getting towards morning we go back to where we started off."

Magee understood straight away. "If you'd stayed in

your proper room all night and those two myalls came back trying to rescue Inkerman you could have been speared in your sleep."

It only dawned on me then that the Boss had been afraid all the time that one of the station gins would tell the two myalls where we slept. You never knew what was going on among the blacks out there in the bush. All that business with the beds was an old bushman's trick going back to the early days. The blacks normally attacked before daylight, and experienced bushmen got into the habit of making camp in one spot and then, after dark, taking a blanket and sleeping under a bush some distance away. Many a spear-studded swag testified to the wisdom of the precaution.

Magee's main concern was for the two myalls. "What d'you want to let them go for?" he demanded. "I've been two years looking for that pair."

It turned out that these two blacks had murdered a white man on Koolburra Station about two years before and had been roaming the Peninsula spearing cattle and robbing homesteads ever since.

Another blackfellow who gave us some trouble was George—a real no-hoper if ever there was one. He wandered from station to station, begging, stealing, scrounging from the other blacks, always in trouble and a nuisance to everyone.

While hanging round Mount Mulgrave he apparently decided that Albert had a good easy job and if he could only get rid of Albert he might be able to get the job himself. The first I knew of it was one evening when the men were away and Albert came home without the cows and shaking with fright. "Missus," he said, "no more can bring em cow. George along 'nother side of river. He going to point bone alonga me."

Albert would have done anything for us, but if a blackfellow was told that someone was going to point the bone at him it was no good at all trying to reason with him. This bone they used was a piece of human leg-bone, sharpened to a point and sung over in a special way. A blackfellow did not even need to see the bone pointed at him. Somebody only needed to tell him he had been boned and he would just lose all interest in living and waste away and die. Although Albert had been working among white people for years, the old superstition was as strong in him as ever and nothing I could say would have convinced him that George could do him no harm. If I did not interfere Albert would die.

I managed to get Albert to take me downstream to where George was, and I clambered down the bank to the edge of the water and shouted out, "George, if you don't go away I will send for Magee."

All the blacks were afraid of Sergeant Magee and we had no more trouble with George. If he had stopped to think he would have realized he was not in very much danger, because the men were all away and I had no one at the homestead to send but Albert, who would have been too terrified to go anyway. Even had be been willing, it would have taken him a day to muster horses from the big paddock—he would have needed two of them —and they would both have had to be shod, which would have taken him another day. Then it was one day's ride to Palmerville, another to Maytown, and two days' ride for Magee back from Maytown—six days altogether.

It was just George's bone-pointing bluff against my Sergeant Magee bluff, and George, luckily for Albert and me, was just as scared of Magee as Albert was of the bone.

Strange blacks on the station did not always mean trouble. Sometimes a mob of unusual-looking blacks would pass through with no clothes on, their hair all waxed out, and armed with spears. They never carried any food, just lived off the bush.

I would ask the gins, "What name?" but I never got any information out of them.

"No savvy him, he gone run," was all they would say.

CHAPTER THIRTEEN

❧ ❧

"No More Find em Tim"

I suppose some people today, reading how the Boss handled Charlie Inkerman, would say he was a hard man. In a way, I suppose he was; he certainly never stood any nonsense from boys who tried to make trouble. On the other hand, there were white men he would not work with because he said they were too severe with the blacks. There was a relationship between the Boss and his boys that you could not understand unless you knew the way he had grown up, the blacks, and the country.

The blacks themselves, who were good judges of character, could feel it and they showed time and again what it meant to them. The way Maggie stood by me during the raid was part of it. Wherever the Boss went, boys who had worked for him before followed him and wanted to work for him again. A boy who followed him to Mount Mulgrave after I came was Tim Taylor.

I will never forget one day when the Boss had been swimming a mob of cattle over the Mitchell, which was running pretty strongly at the time. When I met him at the sliprails I could see at once that something was wrong. I said, "What sort of a crossing did you have?"

"We drowned poor old Tim."

Nobody had seen exactly what happened. It had

apparently been a fairly difficult crossing, and Tim, who was the best of all the boys with cattle and generally took the brunt of the work, had somehow come off his horse, got tangled up in some weeds and disappeared.

The Boss never showed his feelings much, but he was very upset about Tim. His friendship with this Laura River blackfellow went back to his days at Strathleven before I knew him, and the two of them together had been through a lot of the experiences that made Charlie the kind of man he was.

From as far back as he could remember the Boss had lived a hard, lonely life. As a boy he had heard incredible hardships talked about as though they were part of everyday life. He took the hardships and solitude of the bush for granted. They had moulded him into what he was and he could not have lived without them. That he survived some of the things he experienced seems almost miraculous.

While he was working on his first station job at Lyndhurst in 1904 he did most of the horsebreaking. Parts of Lyndhurst were stony country and the branding and drafting yards were of basalt boulders built into walls about four feet thick. Once when he was breaking a horse he was thrown against one of these walls and broke his hip.

He never had any medical treatment at all for that injury. It apparently healed up somehow, though all our married life he still suffered from a bad back. Years later, just before his last illness, he was X-rayed and the doctor showed me the pictures. His whole right hip seemed to have been smashed right in. How he ever walked with it, let alone toiled and lifted and broke in horses the way he did, I shall never know. He had lived with that injury since he was twenty-one.

In 1906 he had been offered the job of head stockman on Wrotham Park, and the following year, when the Munro-Gordon partnership that owned Wrotham Park bought Koolburra Station from the Fox family, Charlie was sent with a team of black boys 150 miles north to take delivery and have a bangtail muster. A bangtail muster was a count of every beast on a property, and every one of them had to be yarded and have its tail cropped to show it had been counted. In rough country such a muster was a long, hard job.

Horses were bringing a good price at this time, and Charlie had been told after the muster was over to take the boys out brumby-running. That part of the Peninsula was overrun with brumby herds descended from packhorses that had run loose on the rich Laura River grass flats after the packing business to the goldfields died out.

The brumbies were rounded up, the older ones shot, and the best of the young ones broken and handled until they could be sent down to Wrotham Park for sale, many as remounts for the Indian Army.

Life was tough on Koolburra. In spite of Terrible Jimmy's earlier activities, Koolburra was still a dreadful place for wild blacks. White men had to carry rifles all the time and could never relax for a moment. The homestead was a small, two-roomed building of galvanized iron with antbed verandas at back and front and a bark-roofed kitchen. About a hundred yards away was Harry Jones's original slab hut, still standing.

The mailman came up from Laura and went on to Coen. One week he did not turn up at Coen. Police went out and found he must have died of fever on the track and wild pigs had found and eaten him. Mailbags and mail were scattered over a wide area. A large part of the Peninsula was overrun by these pigs, big Captain Cookers, which over the years had grown huge and ferocious.

One of Charlie's best boys at Koolburra was Sandy Cook, who had been brought up by Jim Fox's parents from the Atherton Tableland. That made him as much of an intruder to the local blacks as a white man.

When Charlie sent Sandy to Laura for mail and supplies they waited in ambush and the first Sandy knew of it was a hail of spears. He threw up his right arm to protect his body and received a spear through the biceps. He spurred his horse and galloped clear, broke off the spear shaft, and arrived back at Koolburra with the barbed head still in his arm.

Charlie gave him a good shot of overproof rum, cut out the spear, poured kerosene over the wound to disinfect it, and bound it up tightly to stop the bleeding. Sandy got shakily to his feet.

"All right now, Boss," he announced with a broad grin. "I good now." And he walked away jauntily, his wound forgotten in the comforting tingle of the overproof coursing through his veins.

In 1908, while Charlie was still at Koolburra, Pat Callaghan asked him to manage Strathleven, a wild stretch of Palmer River country downstream from the old gold-rush area. The original run had been forfeited by the de Sallis brothers in 1894 during the slump that followed the end of the rush. Callaghan had taken up part of it under the original name, and J. B. Stewart had taken a block of it farther down the river and called it Drumduff after his home in Northern Ireland.

Supplies came from Cooktown to Laura by train and on to Strathleven by packhorse. The blacks on the Palmer and Mitchell were still fairly wild and detachments of Native Police—generally a white sergeant, white constable and six black troopers—were stationed at Laura, Frome, Highbury and Maytown to keep an eye on them.

Charlie was the only white man on Strathleven and Tim Taylor became his right-hand man among the three black boys who made up his entire staff. While there Charlie got his first bad bout of Gulf fever. He became delirious, could not move or talk sensibly, and seemed close to death.

Under Taylor's direction the Strathleven blacks, with the help of two other station blacks from Drumduff, cut saplings and threaded them through bags to make a stretcher. They loaded the still unconscious Charlie onto it and, while one of them went ahead to tell Sergeant Magee at Maytown, the rest followed in his tracks, taking turns to carry the stretcher.

When they got to Maytown they found the boy who had been sent on ahead had been so sure the Boss would be dead before he arrived that a grave had already been dug.

Finding him still alive, the sergeant sent word to Mount Mulgrave for the buckboard—the same one that I had on my honeymoon—to be sent for him. Mrs Magee in the meantime dosed him with quinine, cleaned him up and fed him on goat's milk and other soft food. There had been a hospital at Maytown during the gold-rush but it had long since been closed.

By the time the buckboard arrived Charlie was still no better and they decided the best thing would be to put him aboard and let the boys take him forty-five miles north to Laura where he could be transferred to the train for Cooktown. So the boys spread Charlie's swag on the floor of the buckboard, lifted Charlie onto it, still almost unconscious, and headed north.

Nobody noticed that one of the bolts in the buckboard was upside down so the threaded end stuck up several inches from the floor. During the jolting journey over stony ground the swag slipped and the bolt worked its way into Charlie's back. He was too sick to know what was happening and it was only when they reached Laura and the blacks lifted him out to carry him to the train that the terrible wound was revealed.

It was a peculiarity of the fever that it generally abated once the sufferer got away from the area where he contracted it. By the time Charlie reached Cooktown he was much better and the main worry was the gaping hole in his back.

Probably because of the poor station fare of salt beef and damper on which he had been living, the wound took a long time to heal, and the proud flesh round it had to be removed by Matron Reynolds with a caustic pencil. When it healed at last it left a permanent hole in his back that I could nearly put my fist into. There was no flesh left and in places you could see the skin and nerves just lying on the bone.

When he came out of hospital Pat Callaghan put him in charge of Mount Mulgrave so Pat himself could make a trip to the Northern Territory to buy bulls and another to Sydney to buy horses. But Charlie's fever kept recurring and all the time he was getting steadily weaker. Dr Khorteum, who treated him in Cooktown, had told him he would never shake off the fever completely without a change of climate, so about the end of 1910 he took the job at Nockatunga, in the dry Channel Country, in the hope of finally getting rid of it.

Tim Taylor returned to his tribe at Laura, saying he would never work for any other white man but the Boss. When Tim heard that the Boss was back at Mount Mulgrave he came down from the Laura and asked for a job.

After Tim disappeared at the crossing the Boss went out several times looking for him, and he would not take any of the other boys with him.

The boys themselves and the gins were out along the river bank looking for Tim. Kitty, always a stickler for ancient Aboriginal custom, kept urging them on, saying over and over again, "Can't leave him, must bring him home."

But they always came back without him and each time they had a corroboree that night about "No More Find em Tim". They kept up the search for weeks.

If they had found the body they would have taken it back to their camp and kept it there for a month or more, singing over it and mourning. It would not have been very nice for me with the gins coming up from the camp to work in the kitchen every day. It would not have been very nice for poor old Tim either. Anyway, they never brought Tim back to the camp and after a while there were no more corroborees about it.

It was not until years later that I found out why the blacks never found Tim, and at the same time why the Boss would not have any of the boys with him when he went out searching. Tim had been buried in a proper grave out in the bush.

CHAPTER FOURTEEN

❦·❦

The Distant Drum

About the middle of August 1914 Jack Burton, of the Palmerville Telegraph Office, sent us word that war had broken out in Europe. That was all we knew until the mailman arrived on Sunday with the newspapers, and it was nearly two months before I got the mail from my family at home.

My father and my brothers Fred and Hugh were in camp, also Ralph, who had left school to enlist as a bugler at the age of fifteen. Rupert and Tim (Aubrey) had already enlisted in Australia. My father later received a letter from King George V saying it had been brought to his notice that he and his five sons had all volunteered for service the day war was declared.

The Boss volunteered at Cairns, but was rejected because of his back injuries. Tom Graham enlisted and left us, and from all the surrounding stations men we knew were answering the call of the distant drum.

The Cape York Peninsula telegraph line became a vital national link, and Arthur White, at the Walsh office twenty-five miles to the south of us, and Jack Burton, at Palmerville thirty-five miles to the north, had to check their sections of it every month and would meet at the crossing below the homestead.

They carried portable telegraph sets with them and when they arrived we would all go down while they threw a wire over the line and took down the latest war cables coming over in Morse Code. The Boss told them always to bring two packhorses. He killed the day they came and we sent them home loaded up with beef and vegetables.

Life on the station went on much as it always had, except that we also did whatever we could to help the war effort. I taught the gins to knit scarfs and socks and I learnt to make beef extract.

Making that beef extract was a long process. After a beast had been killed the bones were put in five four-gallon kerosene tins filled with water and boiled on the stove. The five tins would just fit on the big kitchen range and we would stoke the fire so they kept boiling all night. Next morning we drained about three tins of soup from the five original tins and boiled these all day. By night we would be down to two tins. We kept boiling until we had only half a tin of extract left, and this we bottled warm. It was so thick that as it cooled it set like jelly.

I sent dozens of jars of that extract to the men in France where, according to letters I received, it was very much appreciated by troops who had been lying in the freezing mud all day.

We also made cakes. Having plenty of butter and eggs in season, the only thing we needed to buy was the fruit. The gins thought it was great fun and never tired of beating up eggs. The Red Cross wrote and told me to put in glycerine and plenty of rum. As the rum we had was all overproof, two gallons of it, which cost twenty-five shillings, went a long way. I also put in plenty of treacle to keep the cakes moist, and I heard they also arrived in good order.

Letters from home were depressing. Ilford was being bombed by the Germans in an attempt to destroy the film factory, so my family were in the thick of it. My mother's letters were full of news of farewells to young men I had known who were now leaving for the front. We had letters from Tom Graham, who spent some time in camp in England and visited London on leave. It must have been a tremendous surprise to a man who only a few months before had never seen a town at all.

My brother Tim was in the landing at Gallipoli early in 1915 and after that our letters to him came back marked "Missing". My father went to the War Office in London, and we wrote to Victoria Barracks in Brisbane, but nobody could tell us anything about him.

Disruption of oversea markets by the war led to the closing down of many of the copper-mines which were dotted all over our part of the Peninsula in those days. Some were supposed to have been worked by Germans who got out as soon as war was declared, and many stories were told of strange comings and goings.

There were five men at Wolfram mine, not far from Mareeba—a German, a Frenchman, a Belgian, and two others who could have been anything. The Frenchman was always flying kites and he could play the piano, the German had a wonderful singing voice, and the Belgian collected native weapons, canoes and things like that and had them dumped on the wharf at Cairns to be shipped overseas. I remember one thing he had lying on the wharf for weeks was a whole magnetic white-ants' nest, which had been picked up out in the scrub and with a great deal of care and trouble carted to the railhead for carriage down to Cairns.

These five men always seemed to have plenty of money, though they never did any mining, and every so often they all went down to the Imperial Hotel for a big beano at which the champagne used to flow like water. After war was declared the mine closed down and they all disappeared. Nobody ever knew what happened to them.

Klondyke mine closed down, too, a great blow to the Fergusons at Blackdown because they had supplied the miners and their families with fresh milk every day, as well as salt meat and vegetables.

The O.K. mine had become a ghost town. The owners

closed it down and got out. The miners, left with no pay, no supplies, and nowhere to send their ore, had no choice but to follow them—in buckboards, on camels that had once been used to carry the ore to Mungana, or on foot.

The Boss later got in touch with the owners of some of the deserted buildings at O.K. and bought them up for the timber and roofing iron, and we drove over in the big wagon to collect it. We found O.K. falling to pieces and a real ghost town. People had just walked out of it with what they could carry and left the rest. In the schoolroom there were books lying open on the desks, and in the hospital some of the beds were made up, but others were left as though the patients had just got up and walked away.

The houses we had bought were solid enough outside, but inside nothing remained. White-ants had eaten every bit of pine in them, leaving only the hardwood shells. The hotel was drier than the pub with no beer, but still un-damaged and withstanding the onslaughts of the white-ants was the beautiful cedar bar counter, about fourteen feet long and three feet wide, as solid as the day it was put in. We managed to salvage some solid hardwood and iron and got enough timber to put ceilings at last on our living-room and main bedroom.

The mine shafts were all flooded, but there was still plenty of copper in them apparently. While we were camped there the men tied some old iron bolts in the ends of lengths of string and hung them in the water. They came up coated with copper.

We had some odd characters around the Mitchell in the early days of the war. One Sunday Herb Doyle told us a man riding a bicycle had passed through the Walsh Telegraph Office on his way to Normanton, more than two hundred miles over wild country to the westward, and only a few miles from the coast of the Gulf of Carpentaria. The Whites had told him to take the track through Gamboola which branched off from the Mount Mulgrave track just beyond the office.

The following Sunday Herb told us the stranger had not arrived at Gamboola, so the Boss, thinking he might have missed the turn-off, decided to go out and look for him. He took four boys who were good trackers, all mounted on good horses, and carrying a water-bag, tucker, two sacks and an axe to make a stretcher if it was needed, and an eye-dropper, which past experience had taught him was often the most important item of all in saving a man who had been lost in dry country.

They found the man about twenty miles from the homestead. He had missed the turn-off, branched off into the bush looking for it, and got lost. He was lying, parched and almost dead, beside his bicycle. There was no water within miles. His tongue was so swollen he could not swallow from the water-bag, so while the boys made a stretcher the Boss forced water down the man's throat one drop at a time with the eye-dropper. He kept this up at intervals all the way to the homestead as the boys took turns carrying the stretcher, leading the horses, and wheeling the bicycle.

Though still almost dead when he reached the home-stead, the man improved a little every day, and after about three weeks was well enough to be put on the track down-river to Gamboola. He seemed quite normal once he got over his ordeal in the bush, but all the time he was with us he never told us a thing about himself. He rode off on his bicycle without having told us who he was, what he was doing, or anything else. We never knew his name and we never heard of him again.

Quite a few former miners came through about this time looking for work like fencing and so on. The Boss gave them a job whenever he could, but we never sent them on their way without giving them a supply of flour, tea, sugar and beef.

The Crown Land Ranger, Walter Williams, was very good with a soldering iron and anything that needed mending was always put aside for him to fix when he passed through. He always looked very smart and clean in khaki drills and I especially enjoyed his company because he came from the Old Country.

There were some travelling parsons doing wonderful work in the Mitchell country. I particularly remember a Church of England minister, the Reverend Mr Wilkinson, who went round the stations with his own team of pack-horses and a black boy. He was very good to the miners and stockmen, writing all their letters for them, and he always carried a magic lantern and collection of slides. When he called we would hang up a sheet somewhere so everyone could see and that night there would be a picture show. The blacks, particularly, were fascinated by these.

Mr Wilkinson was almost stone deaf and, this being before the days of electronic hearing aids, he carried around with him a long piece of tubing with a tin funnel fixed to the end of it. When talking to you he would put the other end of the tubing to his ear and thrust the funnel in front of your mouth so you could shout your reply. I remember the first time he did it to Mary; she was not long down from the Coleman River and she came running inside terrified.

Part-owner of Wrotham Park at this time was Jim Clarke, the Pearl King. He lived in Brisbane but made regular trips north to look over his interests. After visiting Wrotham Park he generally came on to Mount Mulgrave for a week's fishing in the Mitchell, often bringing his brother John, who was captain of the coastal steamer *Palmer*, and we got to know them very well.

When Charlie had first gone to Wrotham Park from Lyndhurst in 1906 it was being managed by John Skene, nephew of the part-owner, but at the beginning of 1907 it was sold to W. J. (Billy) Munro, who had a half-share, and John and Robert Gordon with a quarter-share each. Robert's nephew, Jim Gordon, became manager.

Billy Munro, who had butchering interests in Cairns, Mareeba, Mount Garnet and Burbenbank, had made money by buying a share in the O.K. copper-mine from John Munro (no relation) and then selling out for £25,000 before prices began to fall. He already owned two stations adjoining Wrotham Park, Gamboola and Highbury, and he later bought a third, Drumduff, from Stewart.

Robert Gordon looked after the cattle side of the business and his cousin John had his own butchering business. John Gordon and Billy Munro bought up a lot of land a few miles south of Cairns for sugar-cane growing and founded the town of Gordonvale, which was named after John.

In 1909 Jim Gordon, while still managing Wrotham Park, bought into the adjoining property, Strathleven. This sort of thing was not done, and Munro asked him to leave. A man named Roberts took over for a while, but his German wife did not like the climate, could not get along with the blacks, and soon talked her husband into leaving. Roberts was followed as manager by William Evans, who remained until 1913 when Munro and the Gordons sold out to Jim Clarke, Wright, and Ralston. Clarke had the largest share and a lot of the remaining capital was put up by the bank. Ralston became manager at Wrotham Park and the Wrights, with their daughter Dorothy, who later married Walter Lawrence, and son Roy lived at Gamboola, which, together with Highbury and Drumduff, had become a Wrotham Park out-station.

At the time we knew Jim Clarke he was a legendary figure in north Australian waters. He had sold his pearls all over the world and been presented at every Court in Europe. He always wore a black waistcoat in which he carried pearls worth thousands of pounds and he used to bring them out to show us. He rarely lost any, but once in his own drawing-room in his home at New Farm, Brisbane, one of the most valuable of his collection disappeared completely. He dropped it and it vanished.

Only after Jim's death did we hear the sequel to the story of the missing pearl. After he died all his clothes were gathered together and sent to the cleaners before being given away. The missing pearl was found in the cuff of the trousers he was wearing the night he lost it.

Jim was a keen angler and the Boss, who also liked to cast a line when he had time, took him down to a favourite spot on the Mitchell about six miles below the homestead. The Boss made his own minnows by soldering three fish-hooks together and fastening them to a piece of bone or horn about five inches long, shaped and painted to look like a fish, with a swivel at the nose so it would spin. There were plenty of good big barramundi in the Mitchell, and the Boss often had them jump three feet out of the water after his minnow.

He introduced the Clarke brothers to barramundi angling, and first time out they came back to the homestead loaded down with enough barramundi to last the whole station for a week. The biggest of them tipped the scales at twenty-three pounds.

Next day the men all had a spell and Jim gave three gins a sack each and told them to fill them up with mussels from the river. He spent the rest of the day opening the shells and looking for pearls because he said he had once found a pearl in a mussel from the River Dee in Scotland and there seemed to be no reason why there should not be pearls in the Mitchell also.

Jim showed us that pearl from the River Dee, but he never found any like it in the Mitchell.

Towards the end of the year the lineman from the Walsh office arrived with a telegram for the Boss saying his mother had died. Charlie read it, and without saying anything picked up the gun and walked off into the bush. I made no attempt to talk to him. I knew he needed to be alone.

Hours later, when there was still no sign of him, I began to get worried and I found Robin and said to him, "We find em Boss." We followed the Boss's tracks for about three miles until we came to a rocky stretch of the river where he had crossed the stream by stepping on stones. Robin searched around but could not pick up the track. "I bin lose em now, Missus," he said. We had to go home. The Boss returned soon after.

With the war showing no sign of ending the Boss became more and more unsettled. He felt that if he could try to enlist again in Sydney where there would be more men going through he might succeed. We had both been having a bad time with malaria and were due for a holiday. The Boss applied for leave and we boarded the ship south in March 1915.

In Sydney Charlie was again rejected for the A.I.F., which depressed him considerably, though I pointed out that he was doing a vital job on the station. At Dick McManus's suggestion we both had a much needed holiday of about three months and the Boss bought the station a new stallion, Lord Frome, to be shipped north to Cairns.

While we were still in Sydney, with no warning of any kind, I received news that my brother Tim was returning in the hospital ship *Ballarat*, which would berth at Circular Quay in three days' time.

We learnt later that in the landing at Gallipoli a shell had burst over Tim's party and killed thirteen out of fifteen of them. Five days later a truce was called to bury the dead, and one of the burial party turned Tim's body over with his foot and found him still breathing, though unconscious and badly wounded in the head. They took him to hospital at Heliopolis, in Egypt, where he regained consciousness, but not his memory. His identity disc was missing and nobody knew him. In due course he was placed aboard the *Ballarat*, and it was not until the ship was within sight of the Australian coast that he recovered his memory sufficiently to be able to tell the doctors who he was.

We met the ship at Circular Quay, but the crowd was so thick we could get nowhere near it and I was separated from Charlie in the crush. Somebody said the Queenslanders were being taken to Central Station to be put on a train to Brisbane, so I made my way there as well as I could. Charlie found me on the platform and at last we located Tim in a telephone box trying to ring the Halls at Thornleigh.

Tim was still very sick and his nerves were in bad shape, so when we saw him again in Brisbane on our way back north we suggested to the C.O. of the hospital that it might be a good idea if he came and stayed with us on the station for a while. This was eventually arranged after we had returned to Mount Mulgrave, but Tim still needed constant nursing care and he arrived in Cairns in December in charge of Nurse Jeanette Dean.

He was the first returned soldier to reach Cairns, and the Acting Mayor, Alderman A. J. Draper, and the town band were on the wharf to meet him, and as they all marched through the streets to the civic reception women with baskets of flowers scattered them in his path.

CHAPTER FIFTEEN

☜•☞

The Palmerville Races

The outdoor life at Mount Mulgrave did a lot to improve Tim's health and Nurse Dean soon found herself with time on her hands. She loved the life in the bush, and as we had no cook at the time she took on the cooking herself. A name like Jeanette did not seem to fit in with life on a station, and before long we all got into the way of calling her Bridget.

She occupied the spare room I had had built on the veranda, but it became very hot and to get a breath of fresh air at night she moved her bed out under a tree in the garden. All went well until one morning Albert came in and told her, "Missy Dean, come see. Snake track under your bed. Big snake track everywhere. Very big snake, taipan."

Bridget went out and saw in the dust the track of a big snake going under her bed. We had already warned her that the taipan was the most dangerous snake in the north and she was terrified. She had the bed brought back into her room and that night, in spite of the stifling heat, she slept with the French doors tightly shut.

The first we heard of her in the morning was a wild scream, and she came running out on the veranda in her petticoat, white-faced, and clutching her dress in her hand.

"The snake—it's in the wardrobe."

The Boss went in with a stick, Tim followed with a shovel, and after a great deal of thumping they emerged with a huge taipan. Poor Bridget had slept with it shut in the room. Her wardrobe consisted of a curtain hung across one corner, and when she picked up her dress to put it on in the morning, there was the taipan coiled up in the corner.

We measured that taipan and it was twelve feet six inches long, the biggest the Boss had ever seen. Albert and I later skinned it, then salted the skin and tacked it to a board and sent it to the museum in Brisbane. I shall never forget the horrible, sickly smell of that snake. It was the first taipan I ever skinned, and the last.

We always had a lot of snakes at Mount Mulgrave. I became pretty handy with the hoe and killed a lot of them. Once I slept on a death adder. We had camped on Nolan's Creek, and as usual I made a bed by collecting a lot of grass and heaping it on the ground. Next morning, after I had slept on it, one of the men turned the grass over and found the death adder underneath.

Ever since the Boss had been rejected for the A.I.F. he and the Palmer River station men had been planning a big race-meeting at Palmerville for August 1916 to raise money for the Red Cross and Comforts Fund. There were Jim and Ernie Fox of Fernhill Station (no relation of the Fox family at Cairns), Jim Gordon of Strathleven, and Frank Callaghan, an adopted son of Pat, who had taken up Palmerville Station on the northern side of the Palmer and married one of Jim's and Ernie's sisters.

These country race-meetings were a feature of station life. Charlie, when at Lyndhurst, had helped J. H. S. Barnes to establish the Lyndhurst Picnic Race Club, which itself had been the model for the Wrotham Park Club formed by Charlie and Jim Gordon when they were both there.

The prizes—generally consisting of a cup, ladies' bracelets, watches, and silver plate—were usually sent by

Hardy Brothers, jewellers, of Brisbane, to the secretary of the club on approval, and those items not bought as prizes or sold privately by the secretary were returned. The secretary's swag on the way to a race-meeting was often worth hundreds of pounds. As our Palmerville meeting was intended to raise money we had only two prizes, the Palmerville Cup and a Ladies' Bracelet. Everything else went to the Red Cross and Comforts Fund.

There was a mounting buzz of excitement on the station as preparations went forward for the races in September. The best horses were run in and put in a special paddock and their training was begun. All the animals were grass-fed, and competitors were limited to members of the club. Station-owners paid subscriptions for themselves, their managers and stockmen, so everybody soon had a horse in training, and daylight every morning saw them out at the station practice track putting their mounts through their paces.

We had some good horses at that time, and the Boss was training Jumper, his favourite camp horse, and getting his own weight down to nine stone six pounds to ride him. We also trained several other mounts, including Ma Belle, a good racer, little Gay Lass who was not much bigger than a pony, but one of our best horses and an excellent racer, and one of my mares, Mayflower, a tall dark chestnut with a slight blaze on her forehead. Mayflower was a brumby, but as fine upstanding a mare as you would find anywhere. She had been captured on the Palmer from the herd of a beautiful chestnut stallion which had escaped from one of the stations years earlier and gathered himself a following from the descendants of horses brought to the Palmer in the gold-rush days.

Mayflower had never reconciled herself to captivity and was always looking, with pricked ears, back towards the Palmer as though she knew that one day she would be running free with the herd again. Once when they were yarding the horses I opened the wrong gate, the one leading away to the bush. Mayflower saw her chance. She pricked her ears, lifted her tail, and in an instant was through the gate with a thunder of hooves and away. It took the men a couple of days to bring her back.

The riding colours the Boss wore at that meeting were the result of a horseback trip he and I had out on the run to see the green shoot coming through the freshly burned grass. The bright green of the new grass stood out so clearly against the black stubble that the Boss said, "That green on the black would make good riding colours."

So unknown to him, I ordered a few yards of emerald green and black silk and, taking the pattern from colours Mr J. H. S. Barnes had given him at Lyndhurst, made new colours—black with a five-inch-wide green band across the jacket, over the shoulder and down the back. I made a cap to go with it, cutting the peak out of stiff cardboard.

My brother Tim wore Charlie's old Lyndhurst colours, pale blue and white. These had been torn at one time and beautifully darned by Barnes's wife, Sally, who was also very good with horses. She not only helped the men with the stock work at Lyndhurst but broke in her own horses.

We kept all the boys' clothing that had arrived with the winter loading in July for issue just before the races, so everyone had new white shirts, trousers, and elastic-side boots for the occasion. The Boss gave each of them a cheque to spend on the tote or with the hawkers who always gathered at bush race-meetings. I made all the gins new frocks of navy-and-white striped galatea with yokes of red Turkey twill and saw that all the piccaninnies had bright new clothes.

At last the morning arrived to load up and make a start for the races. An extra seat had been put in the back of the buckboard. All our swags and rations had been piled aboard, and Bridget and I climbed up with the Boss, who was driving.

The small wagon, already piled high with tents, food and other gear, pulled up at the blacksmith's shop, and up climbed all the gins and piccaninnies with their own swags and dilly-bags.

Before they were all aboard a difficulty arose. Kitty's latest baby had died two weeks previously, and Aboriginal custom decreed that she should carry the body around wrapped up in bark for several weeks, mourning over it, and then, after a suitable time had elapsed, put the bundle up in the fork of a tree and forget all about it. Kitty arrived to get aboard the wagon still carrying the bark-wrapped bundle.

"You can't take dead piccaninny to races," I told her. "You put em up in tree."

Kitty determinedly shook her head. "No," she insisted. "Me no more finished being sorry. By an' by I finished. Then I put em longa tree."

It was obviously no good arguing with her and none of the other gins seemed to mind, so I let her go ahead, little though I liked the idea of that bundle being carried on the same wagon as a lot of the provisions.

Then we were off, the Boss and I leading the way in the buckboard, gins and piccaninnies following in the wagon, and men and boys all riding their horses like an escort. Just north of Mount Mulgrave we linked up with another party and from there on we made a spectacular showing with our buckboards, wagons, and mobs of mounted men and boys all trailing along behind us, joking and laughing and cracking their whips.

During the day we drew ahead of the heavily laden wagons and reached Palmerville about dark. The wagons came up next day. Buggies, buckboards, wagons and riders had converged from a radius of fifty miles or more, and few of us had much sleep that first night. Everybody just got together and talked and drank tea round the camp-fires. Many of these people had been born and raised in the Peninsula, had never had any formal schooling, or seen a town or salt water in their lives. They were some of the finest people I have ever known.

The once-busy gold-rush town of Palmerville at that time consisted mainly of the Telegraph Office, run by the Burtons, and one of the old hotels, no longer licensed, which was used by Frank Callaghan and his family as their home. There was also Ah Look's store, quite a good and well-stocked one for such an isolated place, and a scattered collection of tumbledown shanties occupied mainly by Chinese still fossicking for a few grains of gold.

We camped at the Telegraph Office to be near the Burtons, with whom we had become friendly, but most of the other white visitors settled in at the racecourse about half a mile further on. It was the only reasonably flat piece of country within miles. The blacks, including all the gins, camped on the opposite side of the river—all except Albert, that is.

He was terrified among all the strange blacks. By their laws he was hundreds of miles outside his proper territory and therefore fair game for any local blackfellow with a spear. Our own station blacks had come to tolerate him because they knew they had to, but there were many blacks gathered at Palmerville for the races who would be glad of the opportunity to see that black justice was done.

Albert stuck very close to us all the time and when we pitched our tent for the night and unrolled our swags on the ground he asked if he could sleep outside the opening. We said he could, and before I went to sleep that night I saw his head just inside the flap of the tent, quite still as he pretended to be asleep, no doubt hoping we would not see him and send him away. When I woke in the morning, there was the Boss on one side of me and Albert, sound asleep, on the other.

Racing arrangements were in the hands of Jim Gordon, who was president—under the guidance of Charlie, who had a copy of the old Lyndhurst rules with him—Ernie Fox, who was secretary until he got drunk and retired, and a committee made up of Jim Fox, Frank Callaghan, and Bob Jenkins, a blacksmith and former gold-mining mate of Tom Graham's. There was to be two days' racing, with races before and after lunch, special races for the boys, foot races for the gins and piccaninnies, and a big social gathering every night.

All the men were at work getting the track in order, clearing tree branches and cutting down undergrowth along the course, putting up rails, building sheds of boughs, carting firewood and filling up old water tanks from the river. For the tote they cut saplings and lashed them together with rope and wire to make the framework, then roofed and closed in three sides with small, leafy saplings. The counter was an old sheet of galvanized iron. The grandstand had a sapling frame, leaf roof, and kerosene cases to sit on.

The women had all brought fruit-cakes, which they were raffling to raise extra funds for the Red Cross and Comforts Fund. The hawkers were doing lively business among the blacks, who clustered round their wagons to buy knives and fishing lines and all kinds of rubbish like gaudy ties and things they did not even know how to wear. Finlay bought a pair of trousers with a bright-red stripe down each leg. A lot of the gins bought themselves straw boaters and before long all of them were decked out like parakeets.

Kitty was carrying the bundle with her dead piccaninny with her wherever she went. The previous night all the blacks had had a big corroboree about it. That parcel came back from the races with her, but after that I lost track of it.

That night we all went to a big corroboree and singsong put on by the blacks, and daylight next morning saw the whole camp astir and buzzing with anticipation.

There were no bookmakers operating on the course and it had been arranged that Tim should run the tote, but so as to have an interest in the racing he rode a Mount Mulgrave horse in the first race, which started at ten. Nobody gave him or his horse a chance; he did not have a ticket on himself and neither did anyone else. He did not get a particularly good start and in a bunched-up field he was soon lost to sight.

The track, though it was the flattest piece of ground for miles round, was far from level, and coming up the straight there was a deep gully where, at a critical stage in the running, all the horses disappeared from sight. On the last lap the field came up the straight and disappeared into the gully. When they came in sight again who should be leading but Tim? He went on to win easily, to the considerable benefit of the tote, but to the chagrin of some who like myself felt too late that they should have backed him.

The Chinese, always great gamblers, had turned out in force. Few of them spoke much English and as they crowded his tote "window" Tim found it hard to understand what ticket they wanted. Most of them seemed to be satisfied with any, and Tim decided to let them have a chance at the long odds by giving them the tickets selling most slowly.

The idea worked at first, but Chinese punters generally follow a rider rather than a horse, and after the second race, the Ladies' Bracelet, was won by Charlie on Jumper, they all decided to follow him.

Tim, who still could not understand what they were saying, continued to hand them out the least favoured tickets. All went well until one of the Chinese thought to compare the number on his ticket with the number on Charlie's saddle-cloth. There was much excited discussion in Chinese and then the whole crowd of them descended on Tim, the spokesman waving his ticket in the air and shouting, "This ticket no good, we wantee Charlie Maunsell." The whole lot of them, a mob of thirty or more, soon made it clear that they felt the same way about it, and the next race was held up while Tim sorted out his book.

A lot of the riders had their own colours at that meeting, and those who did not wore a strip of bright material pinned over their shoulders.

The Boss was generally regarded as one of the finest horsemen and best judges of horseflesh in the north, and there was always a lot of rivalry between him and Jim Gordon. When we first arrived, Jim took one look at Jumper and demanded, "What are you going to do with your cart-horse, Maunsell?"

For months past Jim had been training a horse he had named Verdun after the great battle then recently fought in France, and with this animal he was confident he could beat the best the Boss could come up with. He put everything he had on it and he said to Billy Hodges, "If Verdun don't win, we're done."

Verdun was supposed to be grass-fed like all the other horses, but I am pretty sure he got a good bit of corn with his grass. He embarrassed Jim a lot the night before the race by putting his head into nearly every tent at the track looking for corn. In any event, when the time came to race it made no difference whether Verdun had been fed grass or corn; he followed the Boss's mount all the way, and Jim was "done" indeed.

Strangers with unknown horses were not very welcome at bush race-meetings, and the Palmerville rules excluded them. I remember there was a great deal of discussion among the committee about whether a man from up-river beyond Maytown should be allowed to race a horse he said he had bred himself. The rules were relaxed at last and the committee allowed him to race it, though with considerable misgivings. They need not have worried. The dark horse came in about a hundred yards behind the animal that ran second last.

Billy Hodges was one of those men who had been born on the Palmer and never strayed far away from it. He was shortish in build and wore a broad leather belt on which he carried everything that a man in the bush could ever expect to need—all in little leather pouches he had made himself. One of them contained his watch, which was a huge thing nearly four inches in diameter. Others carried matches, his pipe, a couple of plugs of tobacco, a purse, a bottle of Condy's crystals for snake bites, a castrating knife, a skinning knife, and a lot more. There was not room for one additional pouch. And when he brought his horse up to the starting line, did he take that belt off? Not on your life. The poor old animal had to carry the lot.

The first day we were at Palmerville I heard that old Ah Look, the storekeeper, was very sick and I asked Tim to take me to see if I could do anything for him. He had become a friend of mine through my sending him supplies of vegetables, butter, eggs and, most important of all to him, an occasional kerosene tin of nice clean kidney-fat rendered down and mixed with something to harden it so it was just what was needed for fat lamps. Every time I sent anything to Ah Look I would receive in return a nice little nugget of Palmer River gold as well as delicacies like real China tea, ginger in a jar, and sometimes a large packet of fire-crackers, which we always took over to the blacks' camp at night as a special treat.

Tim and I followed a path among the old huts that still dotted the diggings, passing doors that gave glimpses of dark interiors where old Chinese lay dreaming the time away with opium pipes, and at last, in the Palmerville township itself, found Ah Look's fairly substantial store and living quarters. The old man was sitting propped up in his bed, with no shirt on and obviously close to death. Squatting near the head of the bed was the pigtailed and robed joss-keeper from the Cooktown joss-house, who had been sent for to see what he could do, and filling the tiny room were about twenty Chinamen, apparently from surrounding shanties.

A lot of them had those long steel needles the Chinese use for acupuncture, and every so often, as the mood seemed to take him, one of these men would trot forward with his needle and jab it deep into Ah Look's body while the old man howled with agony. One of them explained to us that they were letting out the devils that were making Ah Look sick. I could not stand the sight of it for long and I told poor old Ah Look that we would come back later.

Ah Look died during the day. They propped him up-right with his arms and legs crossed, on a sort of platform that had handles to carry it by, and about four o'clock in the afternoon some of them picked it up and went trotting off into the bush with it, hard on the heels of an advance party carrying crowbars, picks and shovels to dig the grave.

Beside the body rode the joss-keeper from Cooktown to perform the burial ceremony, and behind followed about six more Chinese carrying articles for the feast that was to be left on Ah Look's grave to feed him wherever he was going. Last of all came the whites—members of the Palmerville Race Club, their wives and families and visitors.

Digging the grave was a slow business in that hard, stony ground, and when it was finished at last, Ah Look was lowered into it, still sitting upright. The dirt was filled in and levelled and the dead man's meal laid out on top of it. There were hams, cooked fowls, rice, nuts, ginger in syrup, Chinese wines, Scotch whisky—everything needed for a feast.

Then we all left. Later on, in accordance with Chinese custom, Ah Look's bones would be dug up and sent home to China in an earthenware jar. But for the present no Chinese would approach the grave for fear of ghosts.

Next morning we heard that the feast that had been left for Ah Look to enjoy in the after-life had disappeared during the night. There were some hard cases among those white stockmen, and they had staged a mighty midnight beano by the side of the grave.

CHAPTER SIXTEEN

※·※

Crossing the Flood

Pat Callaghan, the original owner of Mount Mulgrave, had never married and after his death there was a long delay in finding his relations. He had broken with his adopted son, Frank, after Frank's marriage to one of the Fox girls, and his heirs eventually turned out to be two of his nephews, Con O'Brien, a blacksmith, and Jack O'Brien, a squatter, both of Bairnsdale in Victoria.

Con had come up to see Dick McManus while we were away in Sydney, and after we returned both of them, together with Mrs Jack O'Brien, came and stayed with us at Mount Mulgrave for several weeks.

They were very pleased with the improvements the Boss had put in and the way he had managed the place, but they had decided to sell it and they asked his advice about the sale. He told them the best thing would be to wait until after the wet and then have it auctioned. They agreed and asked him to stay on as manager until then.

It was quite a long time before the sale was eventually arranged, but in the meantime the Boss and I had to look round and make plans for the future.

Tim had already obtained a Soldiers' Settlement block near Millaa Millaa, on the southern part of the Atherton Tableland, and the Boss, in order to have a place to fall back on, bought 140 acres near Malanda, on the Tableland, from Messrs Kohl and Plath, sawmillers, for £7 an acre. Forty acres of it was cleared, the rest was standing timber. There was no house on it, only a shed twelve feet by ten. Bridget did not want to leave the north and began looking for another position.

I was again expecting a baby at the time, and it was good to have Tim and Bridget with us that last Christmas at Mount Mulgrave. Bridget excelled herself by producing a huge three-tier cake, just like a wedding cake. With the wet bringing all the guinea-fowl home we had more eggs than we knew what to do with, the cows were all milking so we had plenty of butter, and everything else was in the store.

She began by breaking sixty eggs into a huge bowl and setting the gins to work beating them while I looked round for three big baking tins. The only thing I could find big enough for the bottom tier was an old prospector's dish. For the next tier we used a big tin I salvaged from the dump, and for the third the biggest of our cake tins.

I could not keep track of all that went into that cake, but I know that as well as flour and sugar there were about five pounds of butter, four large dippers of mixed fruit, two cups of treacle and quite a lot of rum.

The kitchen range had two big ovens, so there was no difficulty with the baking, and all three tiers turned out beautifully. When Bridget put it all together she had to turn the bottom tier upside down because of the sloping sides of the prospector's dish. Then she iced it and the whole thing looked wonderful. The gins and boys all came to stare at it pop-eyed, and next day when it was cut each received a large slice on a plate.

The wet of January and February 1917 was terribly hot and muggy and there was a lot of Gulf fever about. I came down with a bad attack of it, and once again I lost my baby. Bridget said I should see a doctor at once, but it was the middle of the wet and there was no way of getting out from the station.

As soon as the rains began to slacken off in March the Boss said we must get through to Mungana somehow. Bridget would not hear of my attempting to ride a horse, so, although the plains were still a mass of mud, there was nothing for it but to try to get through with the buckboard.

Bridget had obtained a position with Mrs W. C. Abbott at Babinda, south of Cairns, and Tim was anxious to have a look at his block of land, so they both decided to come out with us. We also had with us at the time a cattle buyer, Garnet Evans, and he came too.

Our first problem was crossing the Mitchell. For years the men had been filling the crossing with rocks in their spare time, trying to make it passable in the wet, but the flood was still far too high for it to be forded.

They took the horses over first. The Boss and the boys mustered them in the morning and that afternoon swam them across the river and hobbled them on the other side. The going was sure to be heavy, so they took six buckboard horses and a few more for riding.

Tim and Garnet Evans, meanwhile, took the wheels off the buckboard, made the body into a boat by wrapping a tarpaulin over the bottom of it, and floated it across. The harness and other gear were taken over in the boat. Then the buckboard was reassembled and everything stacked in it and covered up with the tarpaulin ready for an early start in the morning. The horses were left grazing with their hobbles on.

We were up at daylight to put the tucker together for the trip, and after a hurried breakfast were all rowed across the river with the rest of our gear. Then they could not find the horses. A search by all hands disclosed their tracks leading down to the river and the animals were found at last back on the homestead side. They had all swum the flooded stream with their hobbles on, a thing the Boss had never heard of horses doing before. By the time they were swum back again and harnessed up it was well into the morning.

The ground was still very soft and all the way across the black-soil plains to Wrotham Park we were stopping to clean the wheels, clogged with masses of gluey mud up to a foot wide, which had to be chopped away with tomahawks. We reached Wrotham Park by sundown.

The Park at this time was being managed by Blue Whittaker. Ralston had sold his share of the property after earning himself the name of "Old Fireworks" because he had trouble with his staff and always seemed to be firing somebody. Men were coming and going all the time and they used to say that the same horse that brought a man in from Mungana took out another one who had been fired.

Jim Clarke had sent Blue up to try to pull the place together, but Blue had his work cut out. The owners were getting every kind of beast they could off the place to pay off the bank and, in addition, Blue was not familiar with this kind of country. He had been managing Tocal Station in central western Queensland where conditions and climate were altogether different. Expecting a man to come straight from that to manage four big stations like Wrotham Park, Gamboola, Highbury and Drumduff was too much.

Blue had married a daughter of A. C. Grant, who had established the Park, and they had with them their daughter Marcia, then in her twenties. He was always a wonderful host and we all had a very happy evening. He said he himself was waiting for the country to dry out enough for him to get to Mungana where he had to pick up a lead coffin.

After the Wrights took up Gamboola, Mrs Wright, for that first Christmas there, gave her sixteen-year-old son, Roy, a .22 rifle. Anxious to try it out, he had gone straight out with it before breakfast and accidentally shot himself dead with the first shot he fired. The Wrights buried Roy on the station and returned to Brisbane, ordering a lead coffin in which Roy's remains were to be sent down to them. It had arrived at Mungana. Blue decided to come with us to collect it.

We got away early next morning, Blue driving the

Wrotham Park brake, which was bigger than a buckboard and pulled by four horses. Blue thought he was made with that four-in-hand, but driving with him was a hair-raising experience. I was with him once when we had only one of the four wheels on the ground.

This time Bridget and I remained in the unsprung buckboard and Tim and Garnet Evans accompanied Blue in the brake. They had a lively trip. Tim had to unwind Blue's whip from round his neck twice.

Between Wrotham Park and the Walsh River the ground is a peculiar formation of hard, stony ridges and loamy flats generally called spine country, and in the wet season the low ground becomes a quagmire, though its surface still looks fairly firm. Blue had still a lot to learn about it, and as we picked our track among the trees I remember the Boss saying, "Blue is going too low down on that ridge; he'll land in the bog."

He had hardly spoken when it happened. Down went Blue's leaders to their bellies and then the next two floundering behind them, while Blue sat staring in open-mouthed disbelief that horses could sink so suddenly in ground that looked so solid.

The Boss pulled up and all the men gathered round to see what could be done. Blue's horses were unhitched, two long poles were cut and got under their bellies, and one after the other, with a great deal of heaving by all hands and floundering by the horses, the animals were eventually levered out of the mud. Once clear and on a firm footing, they were hitched to the brake at the end of a long pole and so pulled it clear of the bog. I had my camera with me and, sick though I was, I took several photographs of it all.

When we got to the Walsh the river was about thirty feet deep in flood and the flat-bottomed boat that served as a ferry was gone. We pitched a tent, made camp beside the river, and spent the evening discussing whether we should go back or go on. The Boss decided to try to cross.

A bushman always carries an axe, so in the morning

some logs were cut and the horses harnessed to them to drag them to the river. Blue's reins were borrowed and used with ours to lash the logs together to make a raft. Oars were made out of saplings and pieces of packing case. Then the wheels were taken off the buckboard and everything was ferried across in three trips, first the buckboard body, then the wheels, and lastly all the gear and food. The Boss pulled on the oars while Garnet Evans swam behind, holding on to the back to act as a rudder.

Tim, Garnet Evans, and the boys swam the horses over, and then a boat was made by tying our tarpaulin up at each end with a surcingle and wedging a pack-saddle as close to the tie as possible. Bridget and I were got aboard, told not to move a muscle or we would go into the river, and the boat was pushed off, the Boss swimming ahead and towing it by the forward surcingle, and Tim behind to keep it steady. The crossing was made safely, everything was reassembled, and we were on our way again.

Blue decided to wait and we left him with a week's supply of tucker to see him through until the river dropped. He had with him two good black boys, Bricky and Mitchell, to drive the spare horses and help load the heavy lead coffin when he picked it up. We learnt later that he collected the coffin at Mungana and headed back to Wrotham Park with it, but at Nolan's Creek, with Blue driving like mad, the four-in-hand overturned and dumped it in the flood. Bricky dived down and tied the reins to it and with much straining and sliding the horses managed to pull it clear, eventually to be delivered at Gamboola.

I went into hospital at Atherton on the Tableland that time, and after I was discharged the Boss rented a house at Malanda and we had a holiday there to help me shake off the effects of the fever.

While we were there I received a cable saying my brother Hugh had been killed during his last hours of flying before qualifying as a pilot officer in the Royal Flying Corps. The plane in which he had been training had hit an air pocket and he was thrown forward onto the machine-gun, which was mounted right in front of him. Later, when I went home to England, I saw the plane in a display at the Crystal Palace. It was a flimsy-looking thing, just like a child's high chair with wings on it.

Charlie went to Townsville for the auction of Mount Mulgrave because the O'Briens had asked him to be there in case any questions arose with which he could help. The place was sold to William Laughton and Sons for £35,000 and the new owners asked him to stay on for a few months to show them round and help with a bangtail muster. The O'Briens had already given Charlie all his racehorses and twenty heifers from Mount Mulgrave to make a start on the farm, and we decided the best thing would be for me to go out to the farm, taking Albert and Mary with me to help, and start getting the place into shape.

I loved the climate on the Tableland because it reminded me so much of England. Even when the days were hot, the nights were still cool, and the clouds hung so low over the mountains that one could walk through them like the mist on the English moors.

The worst part of it all was having to go back to Mount Mulgrave and say good-bye to all our black boys, gins and piccaninnies. They knew the Boss and I were leaving for good and they wanted to come with us. We had to explain that they were signed on at Mount Mulgrave and could not be released because the new owners needed boys who knew the run, and also that we were going to a farm, which was a very different thing from a station, and much too small to provide work for them all.

Everyone was crying when I left. The only note of relief was provided by Finlay, who for years past had always carried the Boss's swag out to the packhorse. It had always been the same swag, just one blanket, one mosquito net, one change of clothes. This time he looked at it doubtfully, took hold, and could hardly lift it. The Boss, who was coming as far as the railhead with me, had succumbed to some of my ideas since that first fencing trip out to Sandy Creek, and the swag now contained, as well as the Boss's usual Spartan travelling gear, a pillow, two towels, extra clothing and so on. "My word, Boss," said Finlay, grinning, "that's a real married man's swag all right."

CHAPTER SEVENTEEN

❦·❧

Bandicoot Roast

John Atherton, the man who opened the Tableland, had come overland with his wife, Catherine, and family and established his homestead, Emerald End, in grassed bush-land near the junction of Emerald Creek and the Barron River. Soon after, while washing a dish of gravel on the banks of a tributary of the Barron a little farther to the south, he found alluvial tin and, according to one story, called out excitedly to his mate Jim Robson, "Tin, hurroo!" and so gave the name of Tinaroo to a new township that soon grew up there.

Diggers came trooping south from the declining gold-fields of the Palmer and Hodgkinson and, as fresh dis-coveries of tin, gold, copper and other minerals were made, Atherton soon found himself in the middle of a rush that spread south to found Herberton on the headwaters of the Herbert River, west to Irvinebank and south again to Mount Garnet. Their outlet to the sea was Port Douglas, beyond the Great Divide to the north, and the track passed close to Emerald End.

Where it crossed Granite Creek, a few miles south of the homestead, Atherton built the Bush Inn in 1880 to serve the weary and thirsty. Soon stables and a store were built there and the place became the Granite Creek Coach Change.

In 1887 Atherton's son William took cattle west to establish Chillagoe Station between the Walsh and Tate rivers, naming it after a nonsense word that had taken his fancy in an old sea-shanty. About the end of the year a couple of prospectors arrived looking for copper on behalf of John Moffat. William showed them some promising outcrops of ore, and claims were pegged which grew into Mungana and other mining camps.

About twenty miles south along the track to Herberton the township of Atherton grew up, and farther south again Robson's Track, just wide enough for a loaded packhorse, was chopped out of the jungle to the east over the Bellenden Ker Range to Gordonvale, thus giving Herberton miners a shorter outlet to the sea at Cairns. Robson's Track took a more direct line than the Gillies Highway that eventually replaced it and the top section was known as "Over the Bump". Branches led off it to Atherton and places where there was mining.

This southern part of the Tableland, between Atherton and the Bellenden Ker Range, was undulating country, much wetter than around Mareeba, and thickly blanketed with rain-forest which had been growing in the deep volcanic soil for centuries and building up a thick layer of leaf-mould as its trees seeded, died and rotted away to enrich further the soil for their progeny.

There were trees that measured more than twenty feet round their trunks, huge cedars and silky oaks, rosewoods, beeches, walnuts, pines, silkwoods, and a mass of smaller trees, shrubs, vines and creepers matted into a jungle impenetrable except by a few tracks used by Aborigines, who lived well on wallabies, possums, bandicoots and a vast selection of other small game and birds.

In places the forest thinned out into more open pockets, which the Aborigines used for their corroborees, and these gave the first white settlers their foothold. They became staging camps for packers bringing in supplies and taking out minerals along Robson's Track. Yards were built and accommodation provided. The southern Tableland's wet season lasted nine months of the year in those days, with weeks on end of misty, drizzling rain. Tracks were boggy and slippery, and the going was very heavy. Horses often sank to their bellies and an animal that strayed off the track ran the risk of touching a stinging tree, the underside of whose leaves carried poison-tipped hairs that could drive it mad with pain.

A few settlers, Europeans and Chinese, each with little more than a tent, axe and spade, began to fell and burn clearings into the fringes of the jungle and plant corn and perhaps a few vegetables among the fire-blackened logs and stumps.

In 1886 the Queensland Government introduced a village settlement scheme centred round a surveyed village site at Allumbah Pocket, between the crater lakes of Eacham and Barrine on the east and Atherton on the west. Soon the pocket's ancient bloodwoods were being stripped to provide bark for the first settlers' huts. J. M. Roseblade and his son Charles set up the first pit-saw in 1894, Fred Halfpapp opened a store, butcher's shop and post office and brought up a mob of dairy cattle.

Men clearing the scrub, as they called the rain-forest, came out of it torn by lawyer vines and covered in leeches and the mites that caused scrub-itch. Corn crops were eaten by wallabies, bandicoots and kangaroo-rats, and what survived was attacked by cockatoos. The nearest doctor was at Herberton, eighteen miles away, and men hurt while felling trees and women in difficult childbirth died before he could be brought.

Rich stands of silky oak, maple and cedar were chopped down and burnt. The urgent thing was to get the land into production, and there was no local market for timber. Someone tried floating logs down the Barron River, but those that were not pulped going over the Barron Falls were lost out to sea.

The railway from Cairns reached Granite Creek Coach

Change in 1893 and the township was called Mareeba from an Aboriginal word supposed to mean "meeting-place of waters". By 1900 the railway had reached west to Chillagoe and Mungana, and by 1903 it had come south to Atherton. Jack Wassmuth and Neville and Oswald Williamson opened Allumbah's first sawmill.

In 1907 the Government threw open 35,000 acres of the southern Tableland for selection. Farmers came from the Northern Rivers of New South Wales, from Victoria and New Zealand, more jungle fell to the axes, and new towns like Malanda grew up. A pioneer business-man, H. S. Williams, built Allumbah's first hotel in 1907, and soon afterwards the town's name, which led to confusion with the coastal town of Aloomba, was changed to Yunga-burra, from an Aboriginal words meaning "place haunted by spirits".

That first time I went to the farm in 1917, the Boss had seen me on the train at Mareeba with Albert and Mary, and also the twenty heifers and some of the horses the O'Briens had given us. He had arranged for George Plath, of Kohl and Plath the sawmillers, who had the place next to ours, to get the stock off the train at Malanda and have them driven out to the farm, and to take Albert, Mary and me, with all our gear, out on the wagon he used to carry timber.

But by the time the timber wagon was loaded there was no likely place on it to sit, so I told George we would walk behind. "You'll never do it, Missus," he said. "The road is a bog most of the way."

"Then I'll sit on the pole at the back," I told him.

He looked doubtful. "All right, Missus," he agreed at last, "but you'll have to hang on tight."

I settled myself as well as I could on the pole, Albert and Mary managed to climb on top of the load, George cracked his whip, the wagon gave a great lurch, and we were on our way.

It was far from a comfortable trip. Every time George cracked his big bullock whip I thought I was going to get it round my neck. The wagon lurched and jolted, I clung on for my life to the pole, and Albert and Mary rocked from side to side on their own precarious perch on top of the load.

There were times when that wagon had two wheels deep in the mud and the two on the other side up in the air. More than once I was sure we were in the bog to stay, but we arrived safely at the farm at last, and George helped Albert to unload all our belongings and tucker into the shed.

I had a mattress to sleep on in the shed, and we pitched a tent I had bought for Albert and Mary. Then we cut two logs, rested the iron bars of our fireplace across them, and put the billy on. Feeling better now that the fire was going, I cut some sandwiches and, with boxes for chairs, we were ready to begin our pioneering.

It seemed to be raining all the time in those early days at Malanda and finding dry firewood was always a problem until we got into the way of drying it out when we could and storing it under the shed. I later made us all raincoats out of unbleached calico, waterproofed with lampblack and raw linseed oil.

Our shed was twelve feet by ten and about four feet off the ground. Until we could get a house built it would have to serve for almost everything. I did most of my cooking in the open in a cast-iron camp oven, which I had never used before. I soon became so good at it that I even made bread in it. Our rations were brought in by George Plath with his bullock wagon.

Another of our neighbours was Mrs Simms, a daughter of the conductor of the Glasgow Symphony Orchestra. She had married a man her father did not like, and to be rid of them both the irate gentleman had paid their fares to Australia. They had come to the Tableland in the early days, chopped a farm out of the scrub, and raised a hard-working, happy family of thirteen children. Father and boys spent their days felling timber and clearing more land while mother and girls ran the house and milked the cows.

They had a huge kitchen in which, once a month, they held an all-night dance to raise funds for the ambulance. One of the boys played the accordion and a neighbour named Jack Timmins, who had a good voice, contributed comic songs.

Life was hard for women on the Tableland in those days. Every acre of land had to be cleared of timber and thick scrub and then planted with grass before it could be used. Sixty or more cows had to be milked twice a day to bring in a living, and, with the men working so hard clearing land, the women, in addition to doing their house-work and looking after new babies, were always in the cow-yards for the milking. As soon as the young children could walk they were all given their own jobs to do.

The women on the farms may not have had to contend with the kind of loneliness that many women on the out-back stations endured, but, as far as sheer back-breaking work was concerned, it would be hard to find any who contributed more to the opening of the country than those women of the Atherton Tableland. They worked from be-fore dawn until after dark in those days when the scrub was being cleared, and still found time to do work for the community and help their neighbours.

I remember all the time we were waiting for our heifers to calve Mrs Simms sent one of the youngsters over with milk every day, and when they killed a pig we always had pork.

One morning I found all our heifers had gone. There were no fences to keep them in and the tracks that led through the scrub could have taken them anywhere. It was pouring rain as usual, but they had to be found. I could not split up Albert and Mary because they were afraid of the Tableland blacks, so they went off together and I went alone to the adjoining farms asking if anyone had seen the missing cattle. By the time I found them and brought them home at last, I must have walked miles.

After that I decided we should have to put up a fence

between our place and Alec Kohl's, through which they had gone. We had a crosscut saw, maul and wedges, but the timber here was all unfamiliar to me and I had no way of knowing what was best to use. Then I saw a man fixing up a bridge over a creek on the road and I asked him if he would show us which timber to use for fencing. He came and showed Albert what would last longest in the ground.

We measured up some logs of it that were lying about. You had to be careful how you touched a log in those days because there were red-bellied black snakes everywhere. Then Albert and Mary sawed them into post lengths, allowing for two feet six inches in the ground, and we split them into posts with wedges and maul.

I had seen the Boss use sticks with pieces of paper tied round them to look along and get a straight line when making a fence, so I did the same. Albert and Mary dug the post holes, Albert using the crowbar and Mary the shovel. It was a long fence, from the road right across to the creek, so I got them to put in a few strainer posts wherever I thought they would be needed. I bored all the holes for the wire with a one-inch auger and got George Plath to bring out the wire from Malanda. It took us a long time to build that fence, but it was a good one, and it kept the cattle at home.

One day, plodding along the muddy track through our scrub, I met a bullock team pulling a wagon-load of logs and driven by a young man so spotless and clean in fresh trousers and Jackie Howe singlet that I stopped to talk to him. His name was Charlie Davidson, he was just back from the war, and was staying with his sister and brother-in-law and helping out by driving the bullock team.

I met him again several times after that. People all called him Prince. He told me it was to distinguish him because his uncle's, cousin's and his own names were all C. W. Davidson. He was always so neat and spotless that the name suited him. After rising to the rank of colonel in World War II he played a prominent part in the organization of the Country Party, became Postmaster General, and now he is Sir Charles Davidson. But I shall always remember him the way I saw him that first day up at Malanda, spotlessly clean in the mud, and driving a team of bullocks.

The Boss wired me at last to say he was on his way with Finlay and the rest of the horses, and asking me to meet him at Mareeba. He planned to take the horses off the train there and bring them to the farm across country.

Among the horses were his favourite camp horse, Jumper, also little Gay Lass, Ma Belle, and my brumby mare, Mayflower. They had also my brother Tim's two horses and a packhorse and saddle. There were about ten of them altogether. We drove them to a spot about fifteen miles out on Rocky Creek the first night, hobbled them and made camp. The Creek was well named. There were huge rocks everywhere and the only place level enough to camp was down in the bed of the creek beside the running water.

In the morning Tim's two horses and Mayflower were nowhere to be found. Tim's two were back at Mount Mulgrave in less than two days, but Mayflower was gone for good, no doubt back with the brumby herd she had never forgotten. All the way in the train from Mungana to Mareeba, the Boss told me, whenever he went back to check on the horses Mayflower was standing alert, ears pricked, with her eyes on the sun which would show her the direction of home.

When we got to Yungaburra we had a further problem. Beyond the town was dense scrub dotted with stinging trees. One narrow track led down to Lake Eacham, lying blue and placid in the crater of an old volcano, and another went through three miles of the stinging-tree scrub and then on to Malanda, seven or eight miles to the south. The Boss said driving the horses through such a narrow track was out of the question.

He had vivid recollections of a time while he was at Lyndhurst when he, a half-caste boy, and a Chinese cook were bringing a mob of bullocks from Lyndhurst through the Seaview Range to Ingham. Camped overnight at the top of the range, in misty rain, he was riding round the mob to keep them together when his horse brushed against a stinging tree. He felt the sting of it even through his rain-proof mackintosh. The horse was badly stung and plunged frantically. He was just able to drag the saddle and bridle off before it broke away and went crashing through the tangle of vegetation to plunge hundreds of feet to its death over a precipice.

The only thing we could think of, if we were not to lose any more of our horses, was for me to hold them together while Charlie, accompanied by Finlay, led one of them to find a safe track through the scrub. Then, leaving the animal with Finlay, he came back and led the others through one by one.

By the time we had all the horses through it was pouring rain and so late that, to get to the farm before dark and avoid another bad patch of scrub, we took a short cut through Kohl's place and opened up a panel of my good fence. I remember the way the Boss squinted along it to see if it was straight, and how it surprised him to find that it was.

Those bush-bred horses did not know themselves on the Tableland, with the lush green grass and running creeks so clear that you could see every stone in the bottom of them.

Next day, as always happened when the Boss was about, work started in earnest. He was strong and healthy, he ignored the pain in his back, and he believed in working every hour God gave him. All the rest of us had to keep up as well as we could.

We rode to town and arranged for Alby Halfpapp, son of the Tableland pioneer, to build our new home. He came back with us, measured up, and ordered all the timber he needed from Kohl and Plath's sawmill on the adjoining farm. It was a big house, with four rooms upstairs, a twelve-foot-wide veranda all round, and living space underneath.

The posts were twelve inches square and the floor plates of bean, huge timbers that you would never see in a house nowadays.

My brother Tim came and stayed with us for a while before going to start work on his own block at Millaa Millaa, a little over ten miles to the south of us. The heifers were beginning to calve, so he and Charlie put up a make-shift cow-bails and yards. Albert did the milking and we set the milk in tin buckets so I could skim off the cream and make butter.

With the house being built and Charlie, Tim, Finlay and Albert there to get on with the outside work, our 140 acres of scrubland soon began to look like a farm. It more than doubled its size when Charlie bought an additional 152 acres adjoining it, cleared and mostly grassed, for £12 an acre. The two blocks together made a fair-sized farm for that kind of country.

One Sunday soon after we all arrived Mrs Simms sent us over our Sunday dinner, complete with vegetables and everything. It was a delicious dinner and when I took back the dishes I told her what a lovely tender piece of pork it was. She laughed as though it was a great joke.

"That was not pork," she said. "That was bandicoot."

"Bandicoot! Why didn't you tell me?"

"If I had, you wouldn't have eaten it."

Wallabies, bandicoots and kangaroo-rats were still numerous enough on the Tableland at that time to be a pest, but I would never have thought of eating them. The scrub turkeys of the Tableland, plump black birds with red heads, were excellent eating, especially if hung until a bit high, like pheasant and partridge in England.

Our blacks from the Mitchell found the Tableland a tremendously exciting place. There were the Malanda picture-shows which they could walk in to see on Saturday nights, and when the circus came to town that was some-thing they had never even imagined before.

Finlay at that time was about seventeen, and I

decided to take him to the circus as a special treat. The nights were dark and we had to take a hurricane lantern to see where we were walking. The strange animals in the cages were all new to Finlay, and the lions, especially, terrified him.

"My word, Missus," he chattered as he watched them pacing their cages, "I think I go."

I managed to persuade him to remain until the show finished about eleven, and then we had the long, lonely walk home, Finlay in front carrying the lantern. The lions were fed after the show and before we had gone far their supper came on and they started to roar. The sound seemed to echo backwards and forwards across the valley and at every roar Finlay literally jumped in the air with fright. I tried to reassure him by telling him the lions were in cages, but he was terrified and it was only his loyalty that kept him with me.

When we got into the scrub the echoes became louder so that the roaring seemed to come from every side of us, from right on top of us, in fact. Finlay let out one terrified yell and ran, lantern and all, leaving me to find my way home as well as I could in the dark.

Except for the dancing glow of countless fireflies, it was pitch-black in that scrub and I had to feel every step of the way to keep on the track. The Tableland was full of stinging trees and snakes, there were cows and horses sleeping on the track, and every time I stumbled into an animal it would jump up in front of my nose, so that before I got home I was nearly as frightened as Finlay.

While we were on the Tableland the Boss did a good bit of cattle-dealing, and this meant that I was often left with only the blacks for company. Finlay, who was generally acknowledged as one of the best rough riders in that part of the country, made a lot of friends in Malanda and was helping some of the young men break in horses. Before going to town on Saturday nights he would often say to me, "Missus, you want a fowl for dinner tomorrow?"

I innocently thought that he was being given them by his friends. I overlooked the fact that his life in the bush, where we had no neighbours and all the poultry in sight belonged to the station, had left him with rather vague ideas on private ownership of such things. So I always said yes, and we had quite a few very nice Sunday fowls before I realized that Finlay was raiding any neighbour's fowlhouse that took his fancy.

"Where are you getting these hens?" I demanded.

Finlay looked injured and surprised. "Doesn't matter, does it, Missus?" he asked. We had no more poultry that was not our own.

We had hardly settled in on the farm when the Boss had a letter offering him the position of general manager of Wrotham Park and its three out-stations, Gamboola, Highbury and Drumduff.

Blue Whittaker had left and the owners needed somebody who knew the north well to take his place. The large area and the rough nature of much of the country comprising the four stations made them difficult to manage. It was claimed by some that the cattle duffers were doing better out of them than the owners.

Soon after this there was another change of ownership. Jim Clarke sold his share to Wright, who died soon after. Then Tom Purcell, of Galway Downs Station, bought into Wrotham Park with Mrs Wright and became the main shareholder.

Before we could take over the management we had to find a share-farmer and his family to work the Malanda farm, and then make a trip down to Cairns to attend to business and arrange loadings for Wrotham Park. By the time we had finished in Cairns there was a railway strike on and no indication of how long it was likely to last.

We could not afford to delay at that stage, so we telephoned Tim, who had remained at the farm for us, to bring Finlay and two packhorses down to Gordonvale by Robson's Track. Though not nearly as much used as it had been before the railway was opened, this track still remained the Tableland's main road link with the coast.

We met Tim and Finlay at Gordonvale and started off up the old pack track with Finlay in the lead, then Tim, then me, and Charlie bringing up the rear. It was steep, winding, and rough, and so narrow in places that I do not know how the old packers got their animals between some of the huge boulders that lined it. In places they were smooth and greased from hundreds of packs that had rubbed against them.

Towards the top of the Bump we passed a notice saying we were three thousand feet above sea-level, and the going became so narrow that we had to get off our horses, tie the reins round their necks, and walk behind them for about three miles. The track was no more than two feet wide. "Don't look down," called the Boss.

Of course that meant that I had to look down out of curiosity. Right alongside where I was walking the ground just dropped away and fell sheer to the bottom of a gorge so far below that I could not distinguish anything there. I could not see any trees, just a blue haze and vague outlines.

A wave of giddiness came over me and for a moment I thought I was going over. Then I managed to look away and take another step. After that I was all right. I had to be. The Boss had no time for that sort of nonsense. At last the ground broadened out underfoot and after a while Finlay was able to hold the horses while we came up with him and mounted them again.

In 1970 when my son was driving me down the Gillies Highway I recognized that spot and pointed up to a mountain ridge high above us and said, "See that ridge up there? That's my track."

CHAPTER EIGHTEEN

※◆※

Life at the Park

Life at Wrotham Park was altogether different from what it had been at Mount Mulgrave. We had a large staff of good, reliable men, and though the Boss worked as hard as ever I saw much more of him and it was not nearly as lonely as it had been before.

We had about ten white men outside, including Friday Butcher, who drove the wagon, Les Morton, an old mate of the Boss's, who looked after the windmills and other machinery, Ted Davis the fence man, Peter Cameron the saddler, and Tom Graham's old mate, Bob Jenkins, blacksmith and wheelwright. We also had about thirty blacks who were camped on Elizabeth Creek.

At Mungana, on our way from the Tableland, we had met Jack Hamill, and the Boss took him on as head stockman. He was a splendid cattle-man, a widower, and had a young daughter, Ivy, aged about eleven, who lived with his sister. Jack slept at the homestead and had his meals with us when he was home, which was not very often, because he was out on the run nearly all the time.

As well as the regular staff there were a lot of travellers catered for at Wrotham Park that I never even saw. They were fed in the kitchen and they camped in the men's quarters as a matter of course. When cattle buyers came with their stockmen and boys the place was like a small township.

The worst of the duffing had been going on from Drumduff, and the Boss found the right manager to stop it in old Tom Brooker. He was a hard, conscientious man who kept his run well branded up and did not mind too much whom he offended.

Highbury was managed by Willie Horning from Bowen, a very good cattle-man, who had one white assistant and the rest black boys. Willie was married to a coloured woman and they had two children, a girl who was nearly as dark as her mother and a boy nearly as fair as his father. Mrs Horning did the cooking and looked after things very well. The Boss always said he had no worries about Highbury.

When the station managers came in to Wrotham Park they normally lived at the house, but the Hornings always made their own camp well away from the place. I said to Willie once, "Next time you come in, you bring Mrs Horning with you; she's just as entitled to have a bedroom in the house as anybody else." He said he would, but he never did.

The manager of Gamboola was Harry Rafter. The Reids had left Gamboola to go cane-farming at Babinda, near Cairns, and been followed by Mr Boyd, who remained only for a while before going north. Harry, a first-rate cattle-man and an old mate of the Boss's from Bowen, applied for the job and took over soon after we arrived.

Harry could do anything with cattle and regularly took camp-draft prizes at shows. He was a widower with six children, four girls and two boys, and, though I do not think he knew it at the time, he was already dying of cancer.

During my years at Mount Mulgrave I had stayed at Wrotham Park for only two nights, so when I arrived to take over I did not really know the lay-out of the place. It was a big house on seven-foot-high blocks. Upstairs was a big sitting-room with a large bedroom on one side of it and two smaller bedrooms on the other. It had a veranda all round, and the veranda alongside the two bedrooms was closed in to make three more bedrooms. Underneath the house was a passageway which led through to the covered walk going to the kitchen. On the left of this passage was the storeroom and on the right, the shady side, a sort of rubbish room that nobody had ever thought of using for anything else. The passage in the middle served as a dining-room.

I knew it was no good asking the Boss to do anything about changing this because he had so many other things to do, but it seemed to me that I could make much better use of the rubbish room as a dining-room than leave it as it was, almost filled with old cement bags and coarse-salt bags by the dozen, old saddles, broken chairs, and every kind of rubbish you could think of.

I decided to wait until all the musterers were away before I made the big onslaught on it, but in the meantime, when the Boss and the others were down at the yards, Albert and Mary and I got a little of the rubbish out every day in the wheelbarrow and brought back bricks, which we hid under the remaining bags.

At last the time came when the men went out on a muster. I got all the gins onto clearing out the rest of the rubbish and bringing back bricks while I took a spirit level to the antbed floor. We levelled it off by soaking the antbed thoroughly with water and then scraping it with a board with the spirit level on top of it. Once we had it level we laid the bricks on it to make a good solid floor.

Friday Butcher and Les Morton were at the homestead at the time, so I got Les to cut an opening seven feet wide in the front wall of the room and Friday to take out the whole of its outside wall. Friday was a good deal alarmed at the changes I was making and doubtful about how the Boss would receive them. "Boss'll sack me for sure when he sees this," he kept muttering.

Friday was a real, rugged old bushman, tall—about six feet three inches—and thin, with a grin of mischief never far from his mouth. He it was who was the leading spirit in the plan to devour poor old Ah Look's funeral feast.

Friday had been a teamster and was a well-known grassfighter in his younger days. They used to talk about the time when he and another noted grassfighter named Steve Scanlan fought all day out at Almaden, about forty-five miles west of Herberton. They would fight a round or two, have a bit more beer to get their strength back, and then start again. It was fairly late in the evening when Scanlan got sick of hitting Friday. He said, "If you don't throw it in this time, Friday, I'm going to knock you out."

"You do it if you can, Steve," said Friday, and they were at it again.

Anyway, Steve did knock him out, and they were good friends after that.

Nobody could understand how Friday was always getting into fights the way he did, because he was a happy man and laughed a lot. I think he used to fight for the fun of it. He always enjoyed a joke, too.

One day while we were working I could hear him outside unloading some wood and talking to old Ted Davis, the quietest and most inoffensive man you would find anywhere. Friday apparently did not know I could hear him and his language was becoming more colourful every minute. I said to Albert, "You go and tell Friday Butcher to stop swearing; I can hear him."

Albert grinned and went out, and I heard him deliver my message. There was a pause, and then came Friday's voice raised in pained rebuke, "There you are, Ted, I told you not to go using that sort of language around the place. Now the Missus has heard you."

And there was the day an old-timer came to the store to buy a pair of trousers. The length of the legs was all right, but round the waist they were far too big. I heard the Boss, who was in the store, say, "If you take those to the Missus she will put a couple of pleats in the top for you."

The old-timer apparently had some doubts about what pleats were, because the next thing I heard was Friday's voice, "Just tell the Missus you want a couple of gussets in the top," he said. "That'll fix 'em up." The gussets would have made the trousers big enough for two men to get into.

But as far as my new building job was concerned Friday Butcher was soon as interested as anyone, though he never showed it. I found a gallon of white paint in the store and painted as much of the inside walls as I could. Then we scrubbed the big dining table from the passageway and polished it with the last bottle of beer in the store, a proceeding that Friday saw as something close to sacrilege. I also found two old home-made settees, which I scrubbed up and arranged in the open just outside the room.

I got Friday to go out and cut me some hollow logs— two or three feet long and with as much space in them as possible—and these I filled with soil to put my pot-plants in. I also planted some creepers just beyond the open side of the room in the hope that the Boss would approve and put in some posts for a trellis.

Friday was not at all sure about things. "The Boss said I was to take that load of rations and stuff over to Highbury while he was away," he said. "There'll be the devil to pay when he sees I haven't done it."

As it turned out, the Boss was very pleased with the changes and when he got time he put in posts near my creepers and made a roof of messmate bark across from the trellis to the side of the house. We got some more ferns and plants, made hanging baskets, and soon had a beautiful fernery beside my new dining-room.

The sun went off that part of the house by the middle of the morning and every afternoon we hosed down the brick floor and the fernery and so had a lovely cool room for the evening meal, even in the middle of summer. Some time after this the Boss built a pantry onto the side of the dining-room and put a stove in it so I could do any cooking of my own without having to go into the kitchen. I turned part of the old passageway into an office.

The Boss later sent to the old O.K. mine for some timber framing and galvanized iron and built a big new store, away from the house, with shutters that could be opened to give plenty of light and bolted down for security. We had the drapery store at one end of it and the groceries at the other. Wrotham Park carried enough stores to service the whole district. There would be a dozen of every size of shirt, trousers, and elastic-side boots, as well as plenty of blankets and everything else that a man in the bush needed. We bought brooms, flour sieves and things like that by the dozen.

I was given the job of storekeeper, and Tom Purcell, when he became part-owner, said I was to be paid £2 a week. It was a big job, because all the loading for the out-stations came to Wrotham Park and was distributed from there.

The manager of Burns Philp once told me that Wrotham Park was worth £3,000 a year to them. Jack and Newell's general store at Mareeba would have sold us about £800 worth in the drapery line, and we also did a lot of business with Cumming and Campbell's and other suppliers.

Wrotham Park was only about six miles from the Walsh Telegraph Office and we were connected to it by telephone, which, of course, the P.M.G. Department serviced. But we also had a private line strung from tree to tree out through Gamboola and Highbury to Drumduff, nearly a hundred miles away. The Boss had a portable phone he could link onto the line anywhere, so the stations were always in contact.

Being a private line, this one had to be maintained by ourselves, and after the wet the boys had to ride out along the full length of it, picking up wires where they had fallen to the ground and replacing broken insulators. The power for the line came from home-made batteries using jars of sal-ammoniac and zinc plates, which required constant cleaning to keep them serviceable. Looking after them was my job. This was, of course, long before radio came to the outback.

The Walsh office was still run by the Whites with the aid of a lineman. They now had five young children, and also a governess and the young gin from the Coleman River, whom Mrs White called Mabel. Arthur White had built his own school, complete even to a flagpole in front, and furnished with desks and blackboard from the abandoned school at the O.K. mine. Before school opened each morning all the children had their own jobs to do, including watering and weeding the vegetable garden and milking their large herd of goats. Every killing day Arthur and the children rode over to Wrotham Park for fresh meat.

Before we had been at Wrotham Park for long our old black friends from Mount Mulgrave began to arrive. The first of them were Billy God-help-us, his wife, Kitty, and their family, who had walked twenty-five miles across country. I remember when I heard they were at the kitchen my first thought was, "Oh my goodness, I hope Kitty hasn't got another dead piccaninny wrapped up in bark!"

She had not, and they were all very glad to be back with us. "No more sign on there," said Billy. "Other feller boss no good." His son Monty was old enough by this to go out with the musterers and was signed on with his father.

Next to arrive were Dick, Maggie and Robin. I was especially pleased to see Maggie. She was a real old myall and would never be anything else, but she had been a faithful friend in those early, anxious days and I would never forget her. Dick had a grin on his face a yard wide, he was so glad to be back with us.

Wrotham Park already had its contingent of gins—old Topsy, who spent most of her time down at the blacks' camp, Dinah and Jessie in the kitchen, and two others in the garden. Work had to be rearranged to keep them all occupied, or they would always be fighting among themselves. So I kept Mary and Albert in the house, put Maggie in the garden, and told Kitty to help with the washing. Some were given the job of sweeping the track to the slip-rails clear of all leaves and rubbish, a task they found it impossible to understand. "What for make em sweep, Missus? Before no more like that."

The most unexpected of all the new arrivals was Charlie Inkerman, the boy we had all the trouble with.

"I good feller now, Boss," he announced. "I come work longa you?"

"All right," said the Boss. "You camp longa hut."

After that we had no trouble with him at all and he turned out a good, reliable worker.

We had a Chinese cook and our vegetable garden was a good one, watered originally with water carried from Elizabeth Creek by the boys and gins. Though this water was quite good, the Boss did not like it for drinking, so one of the first things he did, being a good water diviner, was to find water near the homestead and get Roly Bridge to sink a well. Roly found the first stream of water at about eighteen feet. He slabbed it in and went down until he found a second, which was much stronger. But the Boss still was not satisfied and Roly went on until, at thirty feet, he struck a strong stream with a constant flow. They put a windmill on it and also an engine for when there was not enough wind, and after that we had no water problems at all. We planted citrus and all kinds of fruit-trees, and soon had a good orchard.

The Wrotham Park homestead was surrounded by mango-trees which Charlie and Jim Gordon had planted when they were both there in 1906, and in season we always had masses of mangoes, so many, in fact, that they were a nuisance. Flying foxes used to gather for the feast in squealing hordes until the trees were packed with them and we could not sleep for the noise. Smoke fires lit under the trees were the only things that discouraged them.

When the cows were turned out at night they came and gorged themselves on the dropped mangoes and then went back to the yards and chewed their cuds, spitting out all the mango seeds as they did so. Every morning there would be so many seeds in the yard that the gins had to cart them away in the wheelbarrow.

The black boys used to bring me all kinds of things they found in the bush. Once they brought me a young emu chick, which grew up to be such a pet that it followed me all over the place. It was wonderful at rearing our chickens. Left with their own mothers, the chickens were soon killed by ticks, but the emu seemed to be able to handle the ticks and it was the usual thing to see her wandering round the garden followed by dozens of chicks of all sizes. When I sat down she would come and sit near me with all her brood, the smaller ones under her wings, bigger ones on her back, and a whole flock of them huddled all round her.

If we were late getting in to meals and there was food on the table the emu would walk into the open dining-room and help herself. Once there was ox-tail on the table and the emu got the lot. I arrived just in time to see her with the joints of the tail showing as big bumps all the way down her long neck.

The men were not at all keen on the emu because each morning when they wanted to yard the horses, there would be the emu, sitting right in the middle of the gateway, so all the horses would wheel and bolt back into the big paddock. I am pretty sure that emu got a few chops with the stock-whip when neither the Boss nor I was looking.

Among the blacks was old Pluto, a great-grandfather who was always Master of Ceremonies at the corroborees down at the camp, and he had the job of horsing men to and from the railhead at Mungana, taking horses out to them when they were arriving and bringing back the horses of those who were going away. In spite of having done the job for years, Pluto never formed any clear idea of the distance from Wrotham Park to Mungana.

Once the new chum who ran our Malanda farm came to see us and was met by Pluto. When they arrived at the overnight camp on Nolan's Creek the man, stiff and sore from the unaccustomed day's ride, asked Pluto how much farther it was. "Not far," the old blackfellow told him, "maybe one mile." They had, in fact, nearly thirty miles to go. When the time came for the man to return the Boss took pity on him and drove him back to Mungana in the station buggy. Another two days' ride would have been as much as he could take.

When we arrived at the Park the blacks had a camp, built of odds and ends, down on Elizabeth Creek, but soon after we had a visit from a union representative who told us we were required to build proper quarters for them. The Boss passed it on to the owners, who told him to do the best he could. So he and Friday Butcher made two or three wagon trips across to the O.K. mine and brought back enough timber and iron to put up good big barracks—eight rooms twelve feet by ten, with twelve-foot verandas down two sides. Water was laid on from the windmill tank and the building was still handy to the creek for swimming.

The old humpies were pulled down, the rubbish piled up and burnt, and the blacks moved in to their new quarters—families in the rooms, single boys on one veranda, girls on the other. That night they built a huge bonfire and had a corroboree to celebrate. For a couple of days they thought the "big fella barracks" wonderful, but then nature reasserted itself.

When building the barracks the Boss had raised the building on stumps about four feet from the ground to give good air circulation round it, and that, as things turned out, was a mistake. The blackfellows' link with Mother Earth is a very strong one, and our blacks were never altogether at home unless they were in contact with her. They liked to sit on the ground together round their fire and talk and smoke and sing. Before the week was over they had moved out of the nice new barracks with its clean wooden floors and taken up residence underneath it. And there, in spite of everything we could do, they lived from then on, making their fire there, sitting on the ground, nearly smothered by the smoke, puffing their pipes, talking and laughing away as happy as could be.

CHAPTER NINETEEN

❦❦

Steak and Eggs for Sixty

By the end of April 1918 all the out-stations were branded up, the forward steers had been brought to Wrotham Park and put in the big bullock paddock to wait for buyers, and everyone could relax a little. The managers took time off and came up to the Park to train their horses for the Walsh Picnic Races, which were held every May at the Walsh River.

We had had a letter from Frances Hall's eldest daughter, Edith, then a girl of sixteen, saying that Grandpa Hall, who had retired from his position as chief accountant of the New South Wales Railways and was now over seventy, would like to come and visit us. In spite of our fears that the heat and hard life of the north would be too much for him, he insisted on coming and Edith accompanied him.

The Boss was busy getting bullocks away and training his horses for the races, so I went down to Cairns to meet them. I found that Grandpa Hall had a letter of intro- duction to the manager of Burns Philp and another to the Cairns station-master, who insisted on putting a V.I.P. car on the train for him.

Grandpa had Mr and Mrs Hamilton, some friends from the ship, with him, and I met Mrs Woodruffe of

Mungana and two friends of hers who came to Kuranda with us for the first night. The train was packed with people going up for the races, and when I told the Hamiltons what a country race-meeting was like, they said they would like to come, so I invited them.

Grandpa told me to bring any friends of mine to join us in his V.I.P. carriage, so before the train pulled out I walked along the line and found Jessie Ferguson, of Blackdown, and a friend of hers and asked them to join us. I did the same thing at Mareeba and brought back Mr Kearney, the local representative of Rothwell's, the Brisbane tailors and mercers, and Ted Gallagher, the stock inspector, a huge man, standing six feet three inches and weighing about fifteen stone. Both were on their way to the races.

At Chillagoe we were met by the little Abbott buggy the Boss had sent to bring back Grandpa, Edith, and me, and the four-in-hand brake with a camp bed and plenty of blankets for the overnight stop at Nolan's Creek. By this time I had many more passengers than the Boss had counted on, and there was quite a lot of arranging to be done.

Lew Roberts, who had driven out the buggy, rode back on a spare horse and Mr Kearney drove Grandpa in the buggy. Into the four-in-hand, which had three seats, we crammed Edith, Jessie Ferguson and her friend, Mr and Mrs Hamilton, Mrs Woodruffe and her two friends, together with all the luggage and the driver. That left Ted Gallagher and me, and we hired a buckboard and two horses from Percy Parsons's livery stables.

The trouble was that the good station horses from Wrotham Park were in a hurry to get home and set a good pace, while the two hired animals in our buckboard were not in the same class, and moreover were at home already and not anxious to leave it. Ted Gallagher belaboured them in vain, and the two other vehicles were soon out of sight.

When we got to the Walsh the horses refused to ford it,

and we both had to get out and flog them across every inch of the way, with them trying all the time to swing round and get back. "They'll never do the eight miles of sand we've got to cross tomorrow," I told Ted.

We managed to make Nolan's Creek about dark, both still on foot and dead tired from walking and fighting the useless horses.

The others already had a big fire going, and there was Grandpa, sitting on a log with a tin plate on his knees, enjoying a meal of salt beef and bread. After supper, the fire lighting the whole camp with its flickering glow, we sat around on logs and talked, and Mrs Hamilton, who had a lovely voice, sang "When You Come to the End of a Perfect Day" to the accompaniment of her husband's one-string, cigar-box fiddle. I can see her now, standing there in the glow of the firelight. It was the first time she had ever camped out in the open.

We got an early start in the morning, but Ted and I and our jibbing horses were soon left behind. When we came to the sand Ted got out and walked beside them, flogging them along as well as he could. "You stay in the buckboard," he insisted. "You're only a lightweight."

But before long the horses stopped altogether, so I got out too, and we both walked that eight miles through the sand in the sweltering heat, belting the useless horses.

The others waited for us farther on, so we all arrived at the homestead together. I remember the expression on Charlie's face as he looked at our cavalcade and demanded, "Where on earth are we going to put all these people?"

I had worked it all out as I came along. Jack Hamill moved out of the house to the men's quarters temporarily and we gave his room to Grandpa Hall. Jessie Ferguson and Mrs Woodruffe shared a room, Mr and Mrs Hamilton were settled in the sitting-room, and Edith and Alice Rafter, who was also staying with us, and all the other girls shared one room for dressing and had bunks on the veranda.

By the time everyone was settled in the house and men's quarters were both full up, and a lot more of the men, including those from the out-stations, were at the big camp down on the Walsh River where the races were to be held.

Our Chinese cook took one look at the mob he had to cater for, decided it was too many, and cleared out.

"Edith and I will do the cooking," I told the Boss. "How many are there to cook for?"

"You can call it about sixty," he said.

There was nothing for it but for Edith and me to roll up our sleeves and find out what had to be done. The cook, after the custom of many departing Chinese cooks, had cut a good few heads of cabbage and other vegetables to take with him, and had let the yeast bottles go sour. Starting new yeast bottles would have taken about three days, but luckily I knew enough by then to have a couple of spare bottles always ready, so there was not much delay with the bread.

In the meantime all the men stepped in and made dampers. It was interesting to see, because each of them had his own way of doing it. Jack Hamill made a very good damper, but he mixed it so wet that it went into the oven looking more like batter than anything else. Peter Cameron tended to work his dough too much and his dampers were always on the dry side. Jack Gliddon, who had come up from Southedge with Tom Kilpatrick, was an expert damper maker. Getting them all cooked was no problem because the Wrotham Park range had big double ovens, one on either side of the firebox, with room for dampers above and below.

Once the yeast was ready the bread-making was simple because we had a separate brick oven for the bread, and I turned the baking over to one of the black boys named Palmer, who was very good at it. He knew just how long to keep the wood burning and when to take it out, and he mopped out the oven with a fifty-pound flour bag on the end of a pole, which he dipped in a bucket of water, until he had the temperature down to exactly what was needed.

More than thirty loaves of bread were baked at one time. After we had taken them out of the oven with a board about fourteen inches long by eight inches wide on the end of a broom handle, the oven was just the right temperature for a fruit-cake, so we always had cake mixture ready in tins to put in as soon as the bread came out. Then we closed up the oven and left the cakes for three hours to cook.

The Boss killed a beast every day while the races were on, so there was always plenty of meat. It was steak for breakfast for all hands, with plenty of eggs and bacon to help out. In spite of all the help Edith, Alice Rafter and I could get, that meal seemed to be never-ending. We had two huge iron frying pans cooking breakfast for the men; the black boys and their families took their steak away and cooked it themselves on the ashes of their own camp-fires.

After breakfast was out of the way Edith, Alice and I could begin to think about getting away to the races. It was only a few miles down to the track and the men went ahead on their horses, the white women in the buggy, and all the gins and piccaninnies, clean and colourful in new clothes, piled into the wagon.

Everyone had a picnic lunch at the track and dinner at night was the main meal. It was not nearly such a business as breakfast because most of the men had theirs in their camps at the course. Anyone who was going home at lunch-time would put a great big roast in the oven, so it would be nearly ready when the girls and I came back in the after-noon to help Albert and Mary get everything ready for the house guests. After dinner we would all ride back to the camp for singing and dancing on a big tarpaulin spread out on the ground, to the music of a gramophone and an accordion or two.

During the day we had all the usual race-meeting events, including foot races and gins' races, with Friday Butcher and Bill Bradley, a pair of natural clowns, always on hand to send them off and keep the fun going along the track.

Conspicuous among the throng of shirt-sleeved countrymen was Grandpa Hall in his stiff-fronted shirt and collar and business suit as though all ready to go walking up Pitt Street. Those starched shirts of Grandpa's were our greatest problem of all. He wore a fresh one every day and it had to be ironed exactly to his liking. With those old Potts irons that were heated on top of the stove, the job almost drove us frantic. Mrs Hamilton tried, but he did not like the way she did them. I tried and that was worse. I do not know what would have happened if Albert had not told us he had learnt the way to do it when he was with Dr Khorteum. He soaked the collars and just the front of the shirts in raw starch, left them rolled in a towel overnight, and ironed them in the morning. At last Grandpa was satisfied, and Albert took over the ironing from then on.

Grandpa and the Hamiltons left for home three or four weeks after the races, but Edith stayed on. She loved the bush and was an excellent horsewoman, and she often went out riding with Charlie, who was very proud of her.

CHAPTER TWENTY

❦ ❧

Running the Pigs

In the midst of all the activity at the Park we had a letter from one of our neighbours at Malanda saying that our pigs were getting out of their pens and rooting up all his potatoes.

The Boss was busy and could not get away, so we decided the best thing would be for Edith and me to go over to Malanda and see what was to be done. The Tableland people had problems enough with wallabies and bandicoots eating their crops, without our adding to them with straying pigs.

This sort of thing was a fairly common cause of bad feeling on the Tableland in the early days, and old-timers enjoyed telling the story of two neighbouring farmers who were having trouble with each other's stock straying onto their land. Things eventually reached a point where one of the men, finding one of his neighbour's fowls in his oats, shot it and sent his son over to tell the neighbour to come and remove the body from his farm.

The neighbour had just yoked up his bullock team to snig some logs out of the scrub, so he drove them across to the oats patch and left them grazing on it while he thoughtfully inspected the body of his bird.

Then, with a lot of "Gee there", "Whoa back",

"Over", and "Steady", and much trampling of oats, he at last got the snigging chain lined up to his satisfaction alongside the dead fowl. Hitching the team to the body, he whipped up his bullocks and drove out of the oats in triumph.

At the time we heard about our pigs there was a buck-jumping show on at Mareeba and they were offering a prize to anyone who could stay on one of their horses for two minutes. Riding a buckjumper was nothing to Finlay, so the Boss said he could come along with us to make himself some extra money.

Finlay did even better than he expected. Showmen normally used a flank rope with which they flicked the horses to make sure they put on their best bucking perform-ance. Finlay soon noticed that the flank rope this one was using had tacks in the end of it. The tacks annoyed him and he kept complaining about it so much that some of the crowd joined in. Half-way through the evening the show-man got fed up with it and offered him ten pounds to get to hell out of it and stop spoiling the show. Finlay accepted the easy money and we left.

Next day we took the train to Malanda and walked the four miles out to the farm. Our share-farmer was a "Chummy" recently arrived from England and he knew nothing about handling pigs. He complained that they were always a nuisance, they were going to keep on rooting their way out of the sty no matter what he did, and they were not worth the trouble because they were only bringing twopence a pound anyway. He convinced me at last and I decided the best thing was to get them all off to the bacon factory at Mareeba.

In the morning Edith and I walked back into Malanda and booked a railway pig truck to be ready at the loading ramp at 7.30 a.m. the following day. The next thing was to get a man to cart the pigs in from the farm, but we dis-covered only then that the man who normally did all the pig-carting was out of town.

Somebody told us there was no need to have them carted anyway, because it was quite easy to bring pigs to the railway by leading them with corn. There was plenty of corn at the farm, and this seemed to be the only way out of the trouble, so we decided to try it.

So it was back to the farm again where, with the help of Finlay, Edith and I managed to round up the pigs and, by holding cobs of corn in front of their noses, lead them up the four steps into the shed where we fed them and shut them up for the night, ready to make an early start in the morning.

We were up before daylight to get them moving. Edith and I each had a small bag of corn weighing something over twenty pounds. Finlay had a stockwhip and, of all things, a mouth-organ. We dropped a trail of corn down the steps out of the shed, Finlay opened the door, and the pigs came snuffling out, about thirty of them, all ages and sizes. We continued our trail and everything went perfectly, the pigs all following the corn and Finlay coming behind with the whip to keep them together.

Off down the road we went, sprinkling corn all the way, and this mob of pigs eating their way along in our tracks. Edith, reared in Sydney, was enjoying every moment of it.

Everything went well until we got to the scrub about half a mile from the house. There were morsels under those trees that were more tempting than corn and the pigs went everywhere, rooting into the deep leaf-mould for all kinds of things that grew and lived there, like the huge earthworms up to four feet long and shining in the light in iridescent colours of red, green, and blue. We had to go into the scrub after them with our bags and tempt them out with extra trails of corn, dodging the stinging trees and sharp-spiked lawyer vines as well as we could.

We got them all out and back on the track at last, but then we had to go down a steep hill and cross a running stream called Williams Creek. Edith and I were still leading them with the corn, and as we were going down the hill I looked round and saw those pigs coming down behind us like the charge of the Light Brigade, and Finlay behind them, cracking his whip and blowing away at his mouth-organ as if it was the pipes of Pan.

The creek had a foot or so of water in it, but there was no time to stop and take off shoes and stockings, the pigs were coming too fast. I went straight into the water and waded through. Edith had more time and crossed over on a log.

When we passed the Lowreys', Bert came out waving his hat and cheering and laughing. "If anybody ever writes a book about the Tableland," he told me later, "they'll have to tell the story of how you took the pigs to Malanda."

I had no idea of writing any books about it in those days. The only thing I was concerned about was to see the last of those pigs safely in the railway truck.

They kept us on the trot all those four miles into town. We had to keep ahead of them with the corn trail so they would not scatter. If we did not lay enough they came too fast for us; if we laid too much we were likely to run out of corn before we got to the railway station and then we should have real trouble. The only thing helping us was that as we used up the corn the bags got lighter to carry.

As we came closer to Malanda where the country was more thickly settled, the people at all the farms stopped milking and came out to stare at us.

We reached town just as everyone was out and about, and we had to lay our trail of corn, with that mob of pigs streaming along behind us, right through the main street of Malanda to the trucking yards. Edith and I were dropping corn and calling the pigs, Finlay was cracking his whip and playing his mouth-organ, and every man, woman and child in Malanda was out in the street, to watch us, open-mouthed and hardly able to believe their eyes.

Fortunately for us the truck was at the loading ramp with the doors open and the corn lasted long enough for us to lay a trail up the ramp and into the truck. The pigs all piled in after us. We slammed the bottom half of the divided door, climbed out over the top of it, and thankfully closed and fastened the top door with the pigs safely inside. We were certainly glad to see the last of that lot.

They eventually brought twopence halfpenny a pound, and, after the rail freight was paid, that left about £25 clear, which the Boss presented to Edith and me. He reckoned we had earned it.

CHAPTER TWENTY-ONE

❈❈❈

Cattle-men

Wrotham Park at this time was the biggest cattle station in Queensland, covering, with its out-stations, four thousand square miles of country and carrying 55,000 head of cattle and a thousand horses. Up to three thousand bullocks a year were being sent off it. They were five to six years old, most of them, and averaged a weight of about six hundred pounds each, though there were some real giants among them weighing up to a thousand pounds or more—huge beasts that stood head and shoulders above all the others in a mob.

Our main buyer was old Tom Kilpatrick, who would give us a price for the year's fats, and then come up every two months or so to take them off in mobs of three or four hundred to his own property, Southedge, near Mareeba, where he could hold them until they were ready to be trucked away to the butchers. Because he was able to hold them his prices were generally a bit better than the average, which ranged from £4 to £6 a head. Southedge was good country until about September, but it began to dry out towards the end of the year.

The meatworks at Biboohra, just north of Mareeba, took bullocks while the season lasted, but closed down when it got dry. This meant more work for the musterers because butchers were coming out to the Park every three or four weeks for a few beasts to carry them on.

The normal practice with the stock at Wrotham Park was for all the forward steers, from about two years old, to be brought up from the out-stations, dipped, and put in the bullock paddock. It was a huge paddock, about twenty-five miles square and all beautiful black-soil country. The bullocks were left there to mature until they were ready for sale as five- or six-year-olds.

Suppose Kilpatrick wanted three hundred bullocks, they would yard a mob, he would pick out about that number from the yard, and they would take them about a mile out in the bush to have the count. The buyer and seller, each with two men lined out beside him, would sit on their horses facing each other fifteen or twenty feet apart and the stockmen would drive the bullocks down the lane between them while they counted. For every hundred counted they would call out "One hundred" and tie a knot in their stockwhips. At the end, no matter how quickly the cattle had gone through, they would never differ by more than two or three beasts. Quite often they both arrived at the same figure.

After Kilpatrick—Kil, we all called him—had taken delivery of a mob, Edith and I would often ride out a few miles with them just for the change and to help get the cattle started.

We had staying with us at that time Jack Hamill's daughter, Ivy, aged about twelve and an amazingly capable girl. Not only was she an excellent cook, but she knew all the proper cuts of meat. I used to hear her in the meat house with Edith. "You don't want to cut it that way," Ivy would say. "You're cutting against the grain, you'll spoil it."

We also had Harry Rafter's two young girls, Alice, aged thirteen, and Edie, nine. Harry had to go into hospital at Cairns and he asked if they could come and stay with us. He died of cancer, as I think he realized he would, and the girls were with us for three years before they went to an aunt in Brisbane for the sake of their schooling. The two elder Rafter girls, Myrtle and Dorothy, were working as governesses.

All the girls used to look forward to Kil's visits because he generally brought younger company with him like Paddy Grigan, Charlie Wallace and Jack Gliddon—all grown men, but they were very good to the girls and gave them a lot of attention.

My little stove in the pantry was getting a lot of use because the girls were trying their hands at making all kinds of cakes and things, which they kept putting into Kil's pack-bags as a special treat for him. But he had been in the bush too long for such delicacies and he always pulled them out and handed them back.

"Never let it be said," he told the girls, "that Kilpatrick travelled with cake in his pack-bag."

Kil was in his seventies at this time, still a tough old character with steely blue eyes and a large fund of dry Irish wit. But there was something of a mystery about him. He would never let me take his photograph. He had a stiff arm and I asked him one day what had happened to it. He said he had been shot in the arm, but that was all he would tell me.

In his time Kil had been a great horseman, but now, with the handicap of his arm added to his years, he was inclined to be nervous on a horse and preferred to take things easy on an animal he could rely on.

They told a story about Kil that once he went to the Normanton races with his old mate, Tom Kerr, and Jimmy Stewart of Drumduff, and some of the local men took him down for a large sum of money. When he was leaving they asked him if he had enjoyed himself and would he be coming again. "I'll be back some day when I can get away," he told them.

As soon as he got back to Southedge Kil wrote to his brother in New South Wales and asked him to send up a good blood horse, an unbranded yearling. Kil took the horse off the boat at Cairns himself and brought him home to Southedge for Tom Kerr to train. He branded him with Jimmy Stewart's cattle brand and named him Slow Tom.

By the time Kil, Tom Kerr, and Jimmy Stewart arrived at the Normanton races with him a few years later, Slow Tom was at his peak, though not very well groomed and certainly not looking at all like a racehorse. Tom Kerr rode him, Jimmy Stewart ran a book, and Kil bet fairly heavily.

Slow Tom beat everything in the field without any trouble and the locals lost a lot of money. The three men and their horse left town that night and never went near Normanton again.

Kil was with us in March the night the 1918 cyclone hit us. The winds were tremendous in that cyclone and we thought the homestead roof would go. We had ropes over the corners because it is the corners that generally lift first, and all the black boys pulling their weight on them while we floundered round in the dark and the pouring rain trying to make everything secure.

Suddenly I remembered Kil. He had gone to bed in one of the upstairs rooms and nobody had seen him since. If the wind took the house off its blocks we should probably never see him at all. I clambered up the steps, clinging to the rail to save myself from being blown off by the wind, and went along to Kil's door. The floor was a foot deep in water that could not get away because I had covered the boards with rubberoid, and there was Kil lying on the bed sound asleep. I had to shake him to wake him up.

"Kil, come on out of this," I yelled. "There's a cyclone on." The water was so deep that things were floating round the room. "Come on, Kil, look at the water."

I got him out of the place at last, but he was quite unconcerned about it all, as though a cyclone was the kind of thing that happened every day. We were lucky the homestead survived that blow. Most of the damage was out in the bush. The trees were flattened everywhere and it took all hands from every station three weeks to cut a track through to Mungana. Down on the coast it was even worse. At Babinda, nearly forty miles south of Cairns, the wind blew a railway engine over on its side.

The Reids, who were at Gamboola when we first went to Mount Mulgrave, had used a legacy to buy a sugar-cane farm at Babinda. They had built a lovely new house on it, and Ann went to Sydney for a holiday intending to bring back a gardener to lay out the grounds. She arrived back soon after the cyclone to find nothing standing except the tank full of rain-water. Their new piano was up in the branches of a tree. Jack Reid, who was in the house with his two young daughters, told me that when the front steps blew away he picked up the two little girls, one under each arm, jumped seven feet off the veranda with them, and ran to a culvert under the railway line for shelter.

That was enough of the coast for the Reids. They sold the cane farm, bought Babinda Station, adjoining Wrotham Park, and came back to cattle.

By this time we had another Chinese cook, Jimmy Ah Say, who had cooked for Samuel Maunsell in the Strathmore days. He had come to us from Mount Mulgrave where he had not been happy with the new management. Charlie asked him if the Boss was a "good feller". Jimmy shook his head vigorously. "No good," he said. "He pour out nip of rum, say, 'Good luck Jimmy', and then he drink it himself."

Jimmy was fond of his nip of rum and did not like being left out. Though he liked working for the Boss he could never get over the difference between the hearty cheerfulness of Samuel and the quiet reserve of Charlie, who took after his mother. "Boss too quiet," he told me once. "Father, he haw, haw, haw, laughing all time, not quiet like Boss."

In November 1918 Arthur White phoned from the Walsh to tell us the war was over. The men were all out mustering and the rest of us were so excited that we hung out all the flags we had and played the gramophone continuously. When the Boss came in four days later it was still going and he could not make out what all the excitement was about.

We could hardly wait for mail day to get all the papers. Then, weeks later, there were the letters from home. My mother and father were all right. Of my brothers, one was killed, two were badly wounded, and two came through with hardly any harm.

Later than month Jack Gliddon was at the Park to pick up some bullocks for Tom Kilpatrick. He was a big, heavily built man, a very good sport, and always ready to amuse the girls, with whom he was very popular. The summer storms were late that year and we were having some bad bushfires. One night, after Jack had been fighting fires with the rest of the men and they were all tired, the girls wanted a game and Jack said he would race them to the sliprails and back.

He raced them and won, but he was so hot at the end of it that, before sitting down to discuss the next day's muster with the Boss, he took two bottles of horehound beer and drank them fairly quickly. It was a strong brew that had been working for weeks. The girls and I went upstairs to play the piano and sing.

About half an hour later the Boss came running up to say that Jack had fallen out of his squatter's chair and was unconscious.

We managed to get him onto a mattress on the floor where he could get a breeze, and I put cold towels on his head while Charles phoned Dr Tunstan at Chillagoe. The doctor thought it would be a day or two before he could get away and he told us how to test Jack's limbs. We did so and found his left arm and leg seemed to be useless. The doctor said it sounded like a stroke and that he would come as soon as he could.

For four days Jack lay unconscious with either Charlie or Jack Hamill sitting beside him day and night. Dr Tunstan arrived at last in a hired buckboard with the same two jibbing horses I had helped flog out to the races. He took one look at the patient and said he would not last the night. Jack died a few hours later.

It was very hot weather and Ted Davis made the coffin straight away. The black boys dug a grave and the coffin was put in the buckboard and pulled to the grave by the boys from Southedge Station. The girls all made wreaths out of flowers from our garden.

When we reached the graveside the Boss asked me to find the burial service. While I was looking for it in the Church of England Prayer Book, which was the only one we had, a thought struck me and I said, "I think Jack was a Catholic. Will it be all right?"

"It will be all right," he told me. He had buried men in the bush before without any prayer book at all, or a word said by anybody.

Matron Gliddon, who was a cousin of Jack's, was running her own nursing home in Cairns at the time and she arrived just as we were coming away from the grave. She had come to Chillagoe by train, but by the time she managed to find another buckboard to bring her on from there it was too late.

The great influenza epidemic swept Australia in 1919 and thousands died. The Aborigines had less resistance to the disease than the whites. It was particularly bad in the Peninsula and we were worried about our people. There would have been about fifty blacks on the four stations, a lot of them not officially on the pay-roll but still fed and clothed and looked after.

We wrote to the Minister for Health explaining the position and asking him to have medical supplies sent to us. Next thing a huge medicine chest arrived, together with two white coats, six gauze masks, and a full set of instructions. A number of our boys were sick by then, so the Boss and I set to work at once to read up the instructions and begin dosing the patients with the various mixtures.

The sick Aborigines and half-castes were all brought in from the out-stations, and at one time we had more than thirty patients at the homestead. During the day we kept them out in the sun, sitting up if they could, otherwise lying on home-made stretchers.

The sun seemed to be the best treatment of all and we did not lose one of our blacks. Once they were cured of the flu and strong enough to walk we sent them away on walkabout to recuperate. They had remedies of their own in the bush that would help build up their strength, and we always made it a practice not to interfere with their customs any more than we had to for their own good.

Many other stations did not manage as well as we did and on some, in spite of all the managers could do, more than half the black population died. Charlie and I, right in the midst of it all, managed to dodge the flu during that epidemic. We had a five-gallon cask of overproof rum in the store and every night, after seeing the patients as comfortable as possible, we took a good issue of rum with hot lemon and honey.

It was soon after this that the Government began to implement a policy of trying to make more employment for white men on the stations by taking a proportion of the blacks away and settling them on the Palm Island Aboriginal Reserve. The police would come round regularly and take away so many of the black stockmen and sometimes some of the house gins.

It was a cruel business because it was the younger, experienced workers, who were supposed to be keeping white men out of jobs, that they took away, and this left their parents, and sometimes grandparents, who were living with them on the stations, without anyone to earn money and look after them.

Old Sergeant Magee, who used to come out for them, was just as disgusted about it as we were. He knew our boys had been born on the station and belonged in that country, but his orders were to take so many blacks from each station and that was what he had to do. He used to come past the veranda at Wrotham Park with the poor things and they would look at me and call out, "Save me, Missus, save me." But there was nothing I could do about it and nothing Magee could do either.

We had heard earlier that Tom Graham was badly wounded in the back, and I had written to ask my brother Fred, who was then a lieutenant-colonel, to go and see what was wrong with him and if he needed anything. Fred did so and wrote back to say that Tom was a very sick man and they would be sending him back to Australia as soon as possible. In due course Tom was returned to Australia, and eventually he arrived back at Wrotham Park, still much more ill than he himself realized.

The injury to his spine had affected his brain and he was suffering from delusions of persecution, which made him believe everyone was talking about him, even his old friends. It was a tragic thing because everyone who knew Tom thought the world of him and would have done anything to help him.

Apart from this one obsession, he often showed flashes of his old self, making us all laugh with his stories of how he had walked the streets of London on leave, giving a friendly bushman's good-day to the people he passed. "But do you know," he said, "the people you see in the street over there don't even say good-day to you?"

My brother Fred's visit to him in hospital had puzzled him even more. Why should this Pommy lieutenant-colonel go out of his way to come and see him, an ordinary Aussie private? He said it made him feel very embarrassed and the other diggers in the hospital had ragged him about it for weeks.

We brought Tom into the house with us so we could keep an eye on him, but we could not watch him all the time and he would often wander away into the bush and they would have to track him and bring him back. His feeling that everyone was against him apparently got worse all the time. One day he ran away down the Walsh River and it was hours before we realized he was gone.

All his friends and the black boys went after him to try to find him before he could do himself any harm. They were all bushmen and good trackers, but Tom was a bushman too, and it was soon plain to them all that he was using every trick he knew to give them the slip. He had left the homestead wearing his boots, but before they had followed him far they found he had taken his boots off and was doing all he could to hide his tracks. Time and again they found he had deliberately walked over hard ground or through water. Days were wasted picking up his tracks again.

Every day hopes of finding Tom alive became less. He was obviously completely out of his mind by then and was just running blindly away. The ironical thing was that he was using all his cunning and bushmanship to get away from his friends and they only wanted to help him. But at last even the will to run deserted him and he was found by one of the blacks, miles away from the homestead, just wandering aimlessly. He did not even know where he was or how he got there.

We had to hold him like a prisoner while we got in touch with his sister, who lived at Mungana, and she arranged for him to be properly looked after at the Chillagoe hospital. But Tom died soon after his admission, not far from the country where he was born—the country he had never strayed from except once when duty called.

❦❦

Back to Ballybrood

Towards the end of 1920 Charlie wrote to Tom Purcell to say he would be resigning early in 1921 because he wanted to take me home to see my family in England. Purcell refused to accept the resignation and said the Boss was to take twelve months' holiday on full pay and find somebody to take over as manager while he was away.

As Jack Hamill was the obvious man for the job, we had no more worries and Charlie wrote to Burns Philp asking them to book us a two-berth cabin on a ship that would get us to England in May for the running of the Derby at Epsom, an event he had always wanted to see. We missed it, as things turned out, because the earliest berth available did not get us to England until June.

We arranged to leave Wrotham Park early in March and the week before we left the managers of the out-stations came up to get their rations and talk over the running of the stations while we were away. The last night they were there Jimmy Ah Say gave us our dinner early as usual and Charlie and I went out for our customary evening walk. We had got into the habit of walking out to a ridge about three-quarters of a mile from the homestead to look for topaz. The stones were fairly common in that part of the country and they seemed to show up best after dark, by the light of a candle.

On the way back we noticed the house seemed to be more brightly lit than usual. When we arrived we found every carbide light and hurricane lantern in the place burning, and all hands gathered in the dining-room, which was decorated with streamers and flowers, and the table set with savouries and cakes and a selection of bottles which the mailman must have been smuggling in for weeks.

Jack Hamill took the chair and read a testimonial signed by twenty-two of the staff of the four stations. "We, the undersigned," it stated, "have met this evening to wish you both a safe journey to the homeland and a safe return back to us all at Wrotham Park, and hand you this presentation." The presentation was £75, and as some of the hands received only about £2 a week in those days, it was quite a lot of money.

Jimmy Ah Say had given the blacks a special supper of their own and told them to come to the house when he held up a lantern. They all gathered in the fernery and invited us over to the camp to see a special corroboree they had composed on "Boss and Missus Going Away". Old Pluto was Master of Ceremonies as usual, the men were dressed up in all their paint and feathers, the gins made a chorus and beat time on their thighs with their hands, and the little piccaninnies sat awestruck, the whites of their wide-open eyes gleaming in the light of the fire.

We spent two days in Sydney visiting Charlie's family, including Edith, who had returned to Thornleigh earlier to look after her mother when she was ill, and the five Maunsell aunts, who straight away made sure we would be going to County Limerick in Ireland to see Ballybrood, the Maunsell family home. Each took me aside to tell me how nice it would be if Charlie and I were to have a son to continue the family line.

They explained that the Maunsells traced their family back to a Philip Mansel who had been Cup-bearer to William the Conqueror in 1066, and since then members of the family had distinguished themselves in most of the wars in which England was involved. A Samuel and Phoebe Maunsell had left Ballybrood with their family to migrate to Australia in 1858 and had settled at Brimbin, on the Manning River in New South Wales. Their eldest son, Samuel George, who was born in 1839, was Charlie's father.

On board the R.M.S. *Orsova* we found we were travelling with a number of northern people, including Paddy Reid, a Townsville bank inspector, and also Dr Rose and his wife, a daughter of Lord Charles Beresford, whose estate adjoined the Maunsell estate in Ireland.

We both needed the doctor's help in the Indian Ocean when ten days' rough weather, with deadeyes in the portholes as the ship was tossed by huge waves, brought our malaria back. Then, in the Red Sea, we ran into a sandstorm so thick we could not see the land and the deck hands had to sweep tons of sand off the ship. Along the banks of the Suez Canal British soldiers called out, "Tell George we want to go home." This was, of course, during the reign of King George V.

We left the ship at Toulon in the south of France, booked on the "Express" to Paris, found it was the slow train and changed to the "Rapide", which was the fast one, had a lovely stop-off at Paris, and booked for Calais and Dover. As we crossed the Channel it was a very clear day. Then I saw the white cliffs of England. I could hardly believe that, after all the things that had happened, I was nearly home again.

The English countryside looked unbelievably green and refreshing. From Victoria Station we drove along the Mall. It was dark and Buckingham Palace was bright with lights. The cab put us down at Liverpool Street Station and we took the train to Seven Kings Station at Ilford.

We had radioed our date of arrival from the ship, but there was no one at the station to meet us. Then I saw old Jock, the ticket collector, who remembered me from when

I was a girl, and he told me my father had met every train that day and had only just gone home. Jock piled all our luggage on a trolley and, with a porter pushing it, we set off on foot down the streets of my childhood, where everything seemed just the same as it had always been, in spite of the fact that Ilford by then had a population of 112,000, instead of the 800 it had when I was a little girl.

When we got to the house the porter tipped all the luggage on the front path and Charlie sat on it while I ran to the door and rang the bell and hammered with my fists. Mother opened the door and then my sister came, and then my father. We were all crying and laughing and so excited that we forgot all about Charlie sitting on the suitcases.

I had described him to the family as a typical Australian bushman, and they had apparently expected him to be rather rough and awkward. This tall, handsome, quietly spoken gentleman was quite a surprise to them, and they were all at ease with each other from the start.

While my father and the rest of the family took turns to entertain Charlie and show him round, I was just happy to be home. It was good to be back in a nice big brick house again. It was all just as I had remembered it—the ground-floor frontage, the two bow windows top and bottom, and the staircase leading upstairs. It was a treat to walk on carpets in the living-room and to have a fireplace in every room. Mount Mulgrave, with its doors that opened inwards and holes in the shutters to shoot through, seemed a long, long way away.

We stayed with my brother Fred in Wiltshire, and had some wonderful days around Bath and Bristol, and in the Cotswold Hills. Charlie and Paddy Reid went off to Scotland for two weeks to visit relations of people they knew in North Queensland. Then they crossed to Belfast and wired me to meet them in Dublin. Things were unsettled in Ireland in 1921, and luggage was searched at Liverpool and again at Dublin for firearms.

We saw the Dublin horse show where the horses were the

best Charlie had ever seen. The water jumps particularly impressed him. There was a ditch on either side of a gate and the horses had to clear the lot. He thought the women were better riders than the men. Next to the large ring was a small one where the horses were sold, and anyone could go into the ring and try the animals out. Among the buyers were a number of priests who relied on horses to cover their parishes. They were generally good horsemen and some of them tried out every horse there before making a choice.

Roads and railways had been damaged by fighting between the Irish Republican Army and British troops, and we found the best way we could get round was to hire a taxi for a few days and pay the driver's expenses. About ten o'clock one night on the main road to Killarney we saw the door of a cottage fly open and an old man and his wife came running out waving their arms and scattering pigs and fowls in all directions. "Stop, stop!" they were shouting. "The bridge is blown up."

We stopped and got out of the cab to look. If we had not been warned we should have fallen thirty feet into the river. We found a lane that took us to another crossing.

At Limerick we stayed at the Royal George Hotel, which had sandbags piled round the windows and doorways, and next day Charlie and I went to Ballybrood where the Maunsells lived for four hundred years, though none had been there for nearly a century. It was a stately old house of two storeys with ivy covering the walls up to the roof. The drawing-room took up most of the first floor, and the beautiful old furniture was covered with cream corded silk with a blue Liberty stripe and little rosebuds in shades of pink.

Ballybrood had four hundred acres of arable land, which was rented to pay the rates and a caretaker, Mr Breen, who lived in the servants' quarters and invited us to an Irish dinner of salt beef and damper cooked in the ashes, the same as we were used to having in the Australian bush.

He took us to the stables and showed us an old brougham, a jaunting car, and some side-saddles. There were old-fashioned implements all around the place, and a dairy with benches made of slabs of slate.

We met a very old lady who knew the Maunsells and remembered their leaving. She said the father and mother, three boys and six girls had packed up and gone to Australia in a sailing ship. After seeing the old home they left vacant, one could only wonder why. Charlie could have taken up that lovely Irish estate because he was the heir to it, but not on your life. The isolation of the Australian bush was what he loved, and in a place like Ballybrood he would have felt cramped.

It is too late for the family to claim it now. After the partition of Ireland in 1921 and the subsequent declaration of the Republic in 1937, Ballybrood was taken over by the Irish Government. Before we left the old home I collected a lot of ivy leaves from the walls and when I got back to Sydney handed them round among the family.

Next day we went to Limerick Cathedral and saw all around the altar flags that generations of Maunsells had brought back from the wars. Then we returned round the west coast to Dublin where we boarded the ship for Liverpool. I have always remembered the green fields of Ireland, the flowers, the large hall where I watched four generations dance the Irish jig, the way the peat fires always glowed a bright red until burnt out completely, and the coachman's call echoing round and round the lakes of Killarney.

After we arrived back in England I discovered, to my delight, that I was going to fulfil the aunts' wishes. It seemed that I had to go back to Ballybrood to find the Maunsells an heir.

By October it was time to leave for home. The voyage from Liverpool to Quebec in the S.S. *Minnedosa* was a rough one and I stayed in my cabin most of the time. Charles enjoyed the rough seas and spent a large part of the voyage on deck where freezing waves were breaking and the crew were constantly shovelling off the ice. By the time we sighted the wide mouth of the St Lawrence River the weather was calm and I was on deck as we approached the old French town of Quebec. The maple-trees were all changing colour and their leaves were every possible shade of red, orange, yellow and green.

We toured the sights of Montreal and New York and saw the Niagara Falls before taking the train across the prairies, over the snow-clad Rockies, and down along the Fraser River where the salmon were swimming upstream to spawn. At Vancouver we boarded the S.S. *Niagara* for home.

Though the Pacific crossing was beautifully smooth, I spent most of the voyage in my cabin and had the ship's doctor see me regularly to make sure everything was all right. I was determined to see that nothing went wrong with the baby I was bringing back from Ireland.

CHAPTER TWENTY-THREE

❄❆

"*Bring em Back Piccaninny*"

On our way north from Sydney we stopped off at Brisbane to see our boss, Tom Purcell. He was in his seventies then, and though he still owned two properties in western Queensland where he had spent most of his life, he had just built himself a fine new town house to retire to. It was a treat to talk to a real bushman again.

Tom had started off driving a bullock team and he had never learnt to read or write. He could not even sign his name, but he did know how to get the best out of a property. Since buying an interest in the Park he had paid us one visit, found the place all branded up, and pronounced it the cleanest run he had ever been on. After that he left things entirely to Charlie.

I remember him saying to Charlie while he was there, "Hey, Maunsell, how many bullocks will you get off this year?" Charlie went and looked through the books, checked the rainfall, and worked it all out. Purcell, meanwhile, was making scratches on a tin matchbox with a nail. "I think, Maunsell," he said, "you should get off four thousand this year."

Charlie looked up from his calculations and said, "That's about what I make it." And that was about what it turned out to be.

All his life Tom Purcell never wore a tie or laced up his boots. Finlay asked me who he was, and when I told him it was the big boss he replied, "He old man, Missus; s'pose he'll soon get the pension." Purcell finished up a millionaire.

When we saw him that time in Brisbane Tom Purcell had bad news for us. He was planning to sell his interest in Wrotham Park. It would mean our losing the best boss we ever had.

We arrived back in Cairns early in 1922 and I went into St Anthony's nursing home, run by Matron Gliddon. The Boss had a lot of work waiting for him at the Park and he went straight on. He told me later that everyone, including Darby Riordan, the guard on the train, the Whites at the Walsh, and everybody else, was puzzled to know where I was, but he told them not a word. When all hands turned out to welcome him back to the Park, he told them nothing either. He just handed out the presents we had brought back—accordions, mouth-organs, a new disc gramophone and records, a new white suit for Albert, fishing lines for the gins—and never said a word about me. They all must have been dying of curiosity, but they just kept quiet and waited to see what would happen.

I would have liked to have been there to give the Boss a hand when he had so much to do, but I was determined to stay on in Cairns. I had already lost two babies in the bush and, especially in the wet season, I was not going to go back, get malaria again, and finish up having another miscarriage.

My son Ron was born on 8th May 1922, and one of the first things we did was wire the news to the five aunts, who were delighted. Charlie came down to Cairns, but had to hurry back to the station, though not before he, Tom Kilpatrick, Paddy Atherton, and some more of his mates had a wonderful day wetting the baby's head. At one stage, I heard, Kil bought a bottle of champagne to bring back to me, but the barmaid drew the cork by mistake so the men decided to drink it themselves. I never did find out how they managed to get on the train back to Chillagoe.

Charlie rarely told anybody more than he needed to, and that even included telling people about Ron. When I took the train home five weeks later, and he and Billy God-help-us met me with the buggy at Chillagoe, poor Billy's eyes nearly popped out of his head when he saw me get out of the train with a baby.

We stayed that night at the hotel in Chillagoe and got an early start in the morning. It was too hot for me to hold the baby all the way, so Charlie hung the bassinet at the back of the buggy seat. That night we camped in the open at Nolan's Creek where we had spent so many nights since I first came to the north. It was good to be back in the bush again. The Boss took charge of Ron and put him in a safe place in the shade before he started making the fire and getting supper ready.

I went to work making our bed the way I had learnt to do all the years we had been in the bush—no tent or camp stretcher, because I did not like them, just a proper bush bed. I pulled young branches from the trees and piled them up a foot high. Then I collected all the long grass I could and laid it on top of the branches, flattened it down well and spread the blanket over it.

We both had a swim in the waterhole before supper. I went downstream like any other bushman without stopping to think about it. Then we had our supper and lay down on the bed with our baby between us, our clothes rolled up to make pillows, the clear sky and the stars overhead and the clean bush air all around us. We thanked God for his blessings.

We arrived home on Saturday, very tired, but happy to be back among our friends. Dear old Albert was crying with joy as he watched the Boss hand the baby down to me. None of the gins had seen such a young white baby before and they were fascinated. They kept coming back to have another look at him and grinning happily and repeating over and over, "Missus bring em back white piccaninny."

That night the blacks asked us to come to the creek to see the big new corroboree about the arrival of the first white baby at Wrotham Park.

The news Charlie had kept so quiet now travelled fast and next morning, which was Sunday, Mrs White telephoned from the Walsh office to say they were all coming over to see the new baby. They came driving down the ridge like a cavalcade, Mr and Mrs White and Keith, the youngest, in the sulky, and the other four White children and Grace Main, their governess, riding alongside. The younger White children, much to poor old Albert's disgust, took charge of the baby in his pram while the rest of us sat round and talked all the afternoon. Fifty years later Mrs White still remembered that day, and the way Charlie had said nothing to anyone. "You Maunsells keep a joy very quietly," she said.

We had a lovely Christmas that first year back at the Park. Tom Kilpatrick and his boys were there and there was a big corroboree at the blacks' camp on Christmas Eve. Kil's boys had a special corroboree of their own and you could always tell when they were about because of it.

We all had Christmas dinner together outside in the middle of the day, with a couple of hams, fowls, Christmas pudding and, later in the day, a huge Christmas cake.

That night we all went out to the long bench that the boys and gins used for their meals, and the Boss made them a "Dish of Fire", as they called it. He filled a large enamel basin with raisins, heated them up, poured rum over them and lit it. I remember the way the flames flared up and lit all those startled black faces with big gleaming white eyes all round the long table. Before the flames had died down they were all picking out the raisins and eating them as fast as they could, so that in no time at all the raisins were all gone and everybody was calling out for another "Dish of Fire".

We had one blackfellow named Palmer, who had been

in the Salvation Army, and the others regarded him as a sort of spokesman.

"Come on, Palmer," called Kil. "Make a speech."

Palmer looked about him doubtfully. "Yes, Palmer, speech," said the Boss.

Palmer stood up and looked round at us all. "Mr Chairman and Boss," he said, "we are very happy, thank you very much."

Ever since we had come to the Park we had taken a string of our horses to the Mareeba show. It was a meeting-place for station people for hundreds of miles round, and in 1923 particularly we had a wonderful time. Ron was about twelve months old at the time.

We always took Finlay with us, and as he rode some of our best horses backers sometimes had trouble making up their minds when the Boss was riding in the same event. "I say, Maunsell," came Paddy Atherton's voice as they both rode out, "which horse have you got your dough on?"

Finlay won the figure of eight on one of Charlie's horses that day. Charlie won the camp draft on Jumper, who was seldom beaten in this event at any of the shows. It was a pleasure to watch the way Charlie and that horse worked together, nosing into a mob of cattle to bring out a beast. Jumper only had to be shown the right one; he did the rest.

Before the show was over Charlie had won £75 in prize money and two gold medals, but every time he had a win he shouted all round and he finished up quite a lot out of pocket on the day. But he enjoyed every hour of that show. We both did.

Next day at the races Tom Kilpatrick, a foundation member of the Mareeba Race Club, won the Mareeba Cup with a horse trained and ridden by his old mate, Tom Kerr, who was himself over seventy at the time, but a great horseman. That day the drinks were on Kil—champagne for all, and Kil drinking his out of the cup.

After all the excitement of the week, I was tired that night and I retired to our hotel bedroom and went to bed early. I had not been there long when I heard footsteps I thought I knew coming along the veranda. There was a bang on the door, it opened, and there in the doorway stood old Kil, a little unsteady on his feet because it had been a great day for him, and clutching a bottle of champagne under his arm. He balanced himself carefully and, with a big happy smile on his face, held out the champagne.

"I've brought the champagne, and I want to see the boy," he said.

He came in, looked at Ron, who was sleeping quietly as usual, and announced, "Now, at last we'll have that champagne I intended for you on the birth of your son."

There was a gleam in his eye that looked as if he meant me to finish the bottle with him, but I was not having any of that. "I'll have a drink with you, Kil," I told him, "but you can take the rest of it away."

So we had a drink and Kil, after one more look at "the boy", took his departure. The champagne he insisted on leaving. "You might like a drink during the night," he said.

The men at Wrotham Park were out mustering most of the time in those days because Tom Purcell wanted to get his money out of the property as quickly as possible. We were even selling one and two-year-old steers, and there seemed to be droving plants coming and going all the time.

Tom, as usual, showed good judgment getting out when he did. The 1920s were hard times for most of the northern cattle stations; bullocks were bringing about £2 10s. a head, and we heard that Wrotham Park was one of only about five that were paying their way. Even so, the good days at Wrotham Park were over when Purcell got out. After that we were being pressed continually to make economies, our loadings were cut, the Boss was told to reduce staff, and he had to put off men he had known for most of his life.

At last the Boss had enough of it, and in 1925 he sent

in his resignation. There were no signs of things improving in the near future, he was tired of working for other people, we had Ron to think of now, and the farm at Malanda at least was our own.

Nobody wanted us to go, and when the time came it was hard to leave all the people on the station. We were taking to the farm with us Albert and Mary, and Kitty's daughter Josie, then a girl of about twelve. Dick and Maggie, who had followed us from Mount Mulgrave, wept and begged, "No more go, Boss, no more go, Missus." Jack Hamill, who had come to the Park the day we did, asked for his cheque the day we left, and he rode away from the homestead with us.

I do not think I realized then that I was finally saying good-bye to life on the Mitchell after more than twelve years. I would never know anything like it again.

CHAPTER TWENTY-FOUR

❮❮◆❯❯

The Tableland

We spent nearly twenty years on the Atherton Tableland. They were crowded years of carving a home out of the scrub, Ron growing up, my parents coming from England to stay with us, the war, and working with all the others to keep the farms going and still find time to do something to look after and entertain all the Australian and American troops who were stationed there during the war. They were years lived in a hurry like all of my life, but years with memories that will never fade.

I shall never forget the crisp air and cool nights, the green grass and clear running creeks, and the way the misty rain hung over the mountains as it did in England.

Then there was the clearing of the scrub. In places it was so thick that the only direction you could see anything was up. We took one section of it at a time, cutting out all the millable timber first, and then starting what was called a drive. This was done by cutting all the trees part of the way through and then felling a few along the higher end so they dropped against the partly cut ones below, bringing them down too, and so on until the whole drive was flattened.

When a good acreage was down and had dried out, all the neighbours came and helped with the burning off.

Fires were lit round the outside and burnt in towards the centre, so there was little chance of their getting out of control.

In the ashes of the burn we planted seeds of molasses grass. It was no good as pasture, but it was a rank grower that choked out the weeds before it died back itself. When the molasses grass died we planted Kikuyu grass for pasture. It was already well established on cleared parts of the Tableland, and Charlie, before going off with Albert fencing or clearing, would dig up about three bags of the roots of it and leave Walter, an English lad we had working for us, and me to plant it by hand. This was hot, back-breaking work, and often, on the way home, I would just wade out into the creek and sit down in the water with all my clothes on to cool off.

How I did not die of pneumonia I do not know, but I worked no harder than all the women of the Tableland worked in those days. No matter what happened, the cows always had to be milked, the separating done, and the cream cans ready for Spark McKell to pick up in his truck early in the morning.

The women of the Tableland had a friend they would never forget in Dr Jarvis Nye, who practised at Atherton. Our roads were no more than muddy bullock tracks, but he was always on call. He believed the women worked far too hard, and when he got them into hospital he often kept them there longer than he need have because he knew that as soon as they were home with the new baby or after getting over an illness it would be straight back to the cow-bails for them. No man in the north understood the problems and trials of the pioneer women better than Dr Nye, and no matter how busy he might be from difficult journeys in the mud and wet, his personal interest in his patients was unfailing.

I shall always remember one cold, rainy night when I was in the Atherton hospital recovering from an illness and he invited me home. As I mentioned earlier, he had married

Chum Atherton, and we sat and talked of the old days in front of the big wood fire in the kitchen while Chum basted the roast we were having for dinner and their two sons, Bill and John, splashed each other with water from their bathtub, which had been brought to the fire for warmth.

My mother and father came to stay with us soon after we moved to the Tableland. Ron was only about three at the time, and I remember when I went down to Cairns to meet them at the wharf Charlie insisted I take Josie with me to keep an eye on Ron.

"You'll probably forget all about him, like you forgot about me when you met your father and mother in England," he said.

My parents stayed in Australia about four years. They were with us in 1925 when my brother Tim married Irene Martin, daughter of one of the Tableland pioneers, and still with us in February 1927 when the Tableland was hit by the big cyclone.

That cyclone was quite different from the one we had at Wrotham Park in 1918. There had been a week of stifling hot weather, which was unusual up there, and every day heavy storm clouds built up, covering all the sky but the part of it directly overhead, where there remained a patch of smoky blue through which the sun shone at noon. The heat oppressed everything. Not a breath of wind stirred the trees and even the birds were silent. In the weird stillness you felt you should talk in a whisper.

About noon on the fifth day it suddenly became cooler, and before long it was quite cold. Heavy blue-black clouds came rolling up over the mountains from the south-east right across the sky. "It's coming," said Charlie.

The men covered all the windows, nailed all the doors but one, and we waited on the veranda watching those black, rolling clouds. Suddenly, like a huge tap turned on, the rain came down with a deafening roar. Just as quickly it stopped and there was that same uncanny silence again.

Then we heard the wind coming. In the fading afternoon light we saw it hit the trees in the distance and move across them towards us. With it came rain. We slammed and fastened the door and waited.

The wind and rain swept across us with the same deafening roar as before. We could feel the house shaking. Above the roar of the rain came sharp claps of close thunder and the crash of falling trees.

"We've done all we can," said Charlie. "How about a game of cards?"

So we sat up all night playing bridge, with the house trembling at every heavy wind gust and the rain roaring on the roof so we could hardly hear each other's bids.

Eight inches of rain fell that night, and another seven during the day. Then the cyclone was gone. It left grass, scrub, and trees flattened as though a steam roller had been over them. The ground was a bog and the little creek a raging torrent.

All the clearing that was done to make the farms has completely changed the Tableland since those days. The whole countryside is different—open, rolling fields, bare hills and hardly a tree in sight where it used to be thick scrub and trees all around us. Even the climate is different. Cutting the trees has reduced the rainfall. The soil is drier, the grass dies back more quickly, and there is no longer that almost constant rain that used to annoy Charlie so much.

My mother found life on the farm too isolated and missed the shops, but my father, then seventy-three, fitted in very well. Being handy with tools, he found plenty to do on the farm, and he bought himself a horse, Tommy Ormond, to ride the four miles to the hotel at Malanda for a yarn with the licensee, Jack Hannahan, and other friends he made among the local people.

When he was returning to England father gave Tommy to an old Chinaman who grew vegetables on our farm and hawked the surplus around the town. Delighted with the gift, the Chinaman bought himself a cart, harnessed

Tommy between the shafts, and set out for Malanda in style. Late in the day he returned weary and disgruntled.

"How did you manage with Tommy?" I asked.

"Him no good," replied the Chinaman in disgust. "He no savvy Mrs Tweed, he no savvy Mrs Hensen, he only savvy Jack Hannahan."

Of course, as soon as he reached town Tommy made a bee-line for Jack Hannahan's hotel, pulled up in front of it, and refused to budge, leaving his new owner to carry the baskets of vegetables round town himself.

Charlie still had his good horses and he rode them at races and shows at Malanda and Mareeba. He also did quite a lot of cattle-dealing.

Before we had been on the Tableland long he received a letter from Maddock Hughes of Nockatunga, saying he wanted to start a Hereford herd, and asking Charlie to pick a thousand good one and two-year-old heifers and send them down to him. To Charlie this meant being back with horses, cattle, and cattle-men. He found a man to work the farm and rode off in high spirits.

Ron grew up and started school. It was so wet on the Tableland that Walter Baker, the teacher, asked parents to send their children to school barefoot so they would not have to sit in wet boots and socks all day. Those children worked hard in the cow-bails before and after school, but they had advantages many in the towns did not. Walter taught them to swim in the pool under the waterfall at Malanda, and Les McKeand, champion amateur heavy-weight boxer of New South Wales, who worked for us at the time, taught the boys boxing. Charlie, with the help of Peter Creagh, put in a cement cricket pitch, and a hole in the creek was cleared for swimming. Before Ron went off to boarding-school at Charters Towers we often had as many as six lads staying with us for the holidays.

We killed a beast every fortnight and hung up the four quarters in the meat house. It did not take the boys long to learn where to find the good cuts of meat, and when they got hungry they would come in and cut themselves a steak each and go off down the paddock with bread and sweet potatoes, made themselves a fire, and have a good feed with no trouble to anyone.

Our blacks had left us by then. Billy God-help-us had come to take his daughter Josie back to her people on the Mitchell. Albert and Mary, in spite of their attachment to us, had become tired of the cold and the wet of the Tableland and had asked us to arrange for their return to Cooktown, where Albert wanted to settle.

By the end of 1939 the young men were leaving for the war. Ron enlisted in the R.A.A.F. as soon as he was old enough. His last day on the farm he helped his father with the afternoon milking as usual, and in the evening we all went in to Malanda for his send-off.

All the Tableland boys going away were farewelled. There would be a note in one of the cream cans when Spark McKell brought them back from the factory, saying who was being farewelled at the hall that night. Spark would call at all the farms at 8 p.m. to pick us up in his cream truck with forms across the back of it. The women all took cakes and things, and there was a big boiler the men stoked up outside to make tea when it was not raining; otherwise we did it with an electric urn.

It was pouring rain the night we gave Ron his send-off, but quite a big crowd turned up. Then next morning he was off. I felt the bottom had fallen out of the world.

We had Tony with us at the time. Charlie had applied to the orphanage at Townsville for a lad to help us after Ron went to boarding-school, and Tony was brought up to us by an inspector. He was fifteen and small for his age. He had been left on the steps of the orphanage when a few days old and nobody knew who his parents were.

"You'll find him a bit of a handful," the inspector told us. But all Tony needed was a bit of help and understanding.

All his wages, except sixpence a week for pocket money, had to be paid into a banking account. I soon found out he had always wanted a bicycle and I told him I would help him get it.

There were a lot of bush lemons growing in the scrub on the farm and Tony and I used to pick them. When Charlie was going in to Malanda Tony would take a couple of sugar bags of them and sell them around town. After the Army camps were established on the Tableland he sold a lot of them to the Americans. When we heard of a good second-hand bicycle Tony had enough money saved to buy it. After the lemons were finished there were plenty of Cape gooseberries growing wild. Everyone wanted them for jam, so we picked them and Tony took them to town on his bike and banked all the money he got for them.

As soon as he was eighteen Tony tried to enlist, but by then men working on the land were not being accepted. He was so broken-hearted about it that one morning I told him to get into clean shorts and Jacky Howe singlet. I made up a parcel of clothes and things to tie on the handlebars of his bike and told him to ride down to Innisfail, not to talk to anyone, and get a lift from there to Townsville where he would probably be able to enlist. I gave him his bank book and a few pounds and said good-bye to him with tears in my eyes.

"Remember," I told him, "you are known as Tony Maunsell and the Maunsells have a good name. If you get into the Army I don't want to see one red mark against you in your paybook."

Many months later, when we were in Sydney to see Charlie's sister Frances, Tony somehow found out where we were and came to see us, very smart in his A.I.F. uniform and taller than I remembered him. With a broad grin he showed me his paybook, with not one mark against him. He told me he had got to Townsville safely and, after being accepted for the A.I.F., had given all his savings to an old lady who used to give him food and pocket money while he was in the orphanage. I heard later that he went on to serve in the Korean war and won the Military Medal.

We could not get any help on the farm after Tony left, and Charlie and I worked it ourselves. We used to get up at 4 a.m. and while Charlie was getting in the cows I would do the house. Then, when I heard the engine of the milking machines start, I would go down to the bails. We were milking about sixty cows and it would be about eight o'clock before we were finished. Then we had breakfast and each went about our own jobs until it was time to get in the cows again at three.

Most Tableland people were doing much the same in those days, but they still found time to organize dances and other entertainments for Australian and American troops stationed in the district. One of these was the weekly dance in Malanda when Jack Hensen gave the use of the Majestic Theatre hall free, Ken Sutherland's orchestra played for nothing, eggs and milk came from the farms, butchers provided salt beef, and we raffled fruit-cakes to meet other expenses. After the dance was over and the place cleaned up it was close to cow time again.

CHAPTER TWENTY-FIVE

❧❧

Still in a Hurry

Ron told us on his last leave that he would not be coming back to the farm, so when the opportunity offered we sold it and retired for a while to a small property on the outskirts of Brisbane. Charlie was sixty, I was fifty-six, and the long hours on the farm had become too much for us.

After his discharge from the R.A.A.F. Ron went dam-sinking and then, in 1951, came into partnership with us to buy Rio Station, in the Thompson River sheep country near Longreach in central Queensland.

When word came through that we could take it over Ron was away on a job, so Charlie and I went out, arriving at Longreach in the pouring rain, with the roads more than a foot deep in mud. It was about six miles to the homestead, so when Charlie was offered a lift in a truck he saw me settled in a hotel, took his swag, his dog, and his new Stetson hat, and climbed up beside the driver. They ploughed through the mud for about four miles, but then the truck could get no farther, so Charlie got out, put his new hat on his head, his swag on his shoulder, hitched the dog's chain to his belt, and plodded the remaining two miles on foot, arriving after dark.

With nothing dry enough to make a fire, he had a bite of cold tucker from his swag, laid out his blanket, and bedded down on the floor. Next day I managed to get out with more food and some of our suitcases.

The first thing that hit us at Rio was a plague of rats. They were there in thousands and there was nothing we could do about them. Each night we shut ourselves and our clothing in a different room, but as soon as the light was out we would hear them gnawing away, and long before daylight they would have eaten through the bottom of the door and be all over the place. Dogs and cats would not touch them, and there was little we could do but wait until they moved on, which they did at last, heading north for the Gulf of Carpentaria.

In one respect only did I get the better of those rats. The first thing I did on arriving was start my vegetable garden. The rats ate everything I put in it. Then I remembered that one of the few things a rat cannot take in its stride is mud. So I ran the hose on my vegetables until the whole garden was a bog. Then the rats left it alone.

But worse than the rats that invaded our bedroom at Rio, and even the bats and snakes and wild cats of Mount Mulgrave, was the horde of huge cane toads that I woke up with one morning at Cairns

It was while we were living on the Tableland and Charlie and I were on our way back from seeing Ron, who was stationed at Evans Head in New South Wales at the time. Charlie stopped off at Townsville on some cattle-dealing business and I took his swag and went on to Cairns to stay with Florrie Connors, who lived at the northern suburb of Edge Hill.

Train travel was slow in the north during the war because of all the troop trains and other military traffic on the line, and by the time I reached Cairns it was after midnight. There was no one about and the blackout was on, so I humped Charlie's swag out to Edge Hill where I naturally found the house shut up and in darkness. After all my years in the bush I was used to sleeping in the open, so, rather than wake everyone up, I unrolled Charlie's swag on the lawn in front of the house and bedded down for a few hours' sleep.

I woke up about daylight feeling things crawling over me and, opening my eyes, found I was in the middle of a mass of huge, brown, warty cane toads. They were scrambling over my head, all over my blanket, and crowded all around me on the lawn. There seemed to be hundreds of them. I was still shaking them out of my blankets when Florrie opened the window to see what all the fuss was about.

The Rio homestead was fairly primitive in some ways when we first took it over. The laundry, right out in the yard, was four posts with a few sheets of galvanized iron over the top, a bench with two round tubs on it, and a boiler over an open wood fire. The days can be freezing in Longreach in June, and I used to do the washing with two thick overcoats on over everything else. But once Ron arrived we soon got things in order, and it was good to be back on the land again.

Charlie and I were delighted when Ron and Joan Meekin were married on 17th April 1954, and after that we left Rio for them to take over and retired to Brisbane for the second time. Charlie took up bowling and I went back to working with the Country Women's Association, in which I had been interested since our days at Malanda. It was at this time, too, that we came to know Dr and Mrs Neil Grieve, whose kindness and friendship meant so much to us during our later years.

Later on we were able to look forward to visits from our three lovely, happy granddaughters, Joanne, Margaret, and Barbara, and in 1966 Charlie and I went and stayed with them all at Rio until 1968 when Ron, who had taken an active interest in the Country Party ever since his discharge from the R.A.A.F., won the Country Party plebiscite. In March 1969 we all went to Canberra to see him take his seat in the Senate.

As I said at the beginning of my story, all the important

things in my life have happened in a hurry. I was born in a hurry, I came to Australia in a hurry, I was married in a hurry. I have lived in a hurry and never regretted any of the decisions I made in a hurry. When the time comes I hope to leave in a hurry.

I remember one day during Charlie's last illness, from which he died in May 1970 at the age of eighty-seven. He seemed to have been thinking about something a great deal and he said to me, "You know, after I had seen your home in England, and the kind of life you had led before you came to Australia, I realized I should never have taken you to that life up in the Peninsula—and yet you never complained."

He had such a different childhood from mine that I think he was only beginning to realize then how hard it had been for a girl fresh from England.

"I never had anything to complain about," I told him. "It was lonely at times, but I was happy out there on the station with you, looking after the homestead and the gins, with dear, faithful old Albert, and with young Robin."

I think that made him feel better, and I was able to say it with perfect truthfulness. I had a very happy life in the bush, and if I could have my way there is no place where I would rather spend my last days than back on the Mitchell River with all those good friends I had there.